MEDIA
ECONOMICS

The SAGE COMMTEXT Series

Series Editor:
EVERETTE E. DENNIS
Gannett Center for Media Studies, Columbia University

Founding Editor: F. GERALD KLINE, *late of the School of
Journalism and Mass Communication, University of Minnesota*
Founding Associate Editor: SUSAN H. EVANS, *Annenberg School
of Communications, University of Southern California*

The **SAGE CommText** series brings the substance of mass communication scholarship to student audiences by blending syntheses of current research with applied ideas in concise, moderately priced volumes. Designed for use both as supplementary readings and as "modules" with which the teacher can "create" a new text, the **SAGE CommText** gives students a conceptual map of the field of communication and media research. Some books examine topical areas and issues; others discuss the implications of particular media; still others treat methods and tools used by communication scholars. Written by leading researchers with the student in mind, the **SAGE CommTexts** provide teachers in communication and journalism with solid supplementary materials.

Available in this series:

Robert G. Picard

MEDIA ECONOMICS

Concepts and Issues

Volume 22 **The Sage CommText Series**

SAGE PUBLICATIONS
The Publishers of Professional Social Science
Newbury Park   London   New Delhi

For information address:

SAGE Publications, Inc.
2111 West Hillcrest Drive
Newbury Park, California 91320

SAGE Publications Ltd.
28 Banner Street
London EC1Y 8QE
England

SAGE Publications India Pvt. Ltd.
M-32 Market
Greater Kailash I
New Delhi 110 048 India

Printed in the United States of America

Library of Congress Cataloging-in-Publication Data

Picard, Robert G.
    Media economics : concepts and issues / by Robert G. Picard.
      p.   cm. — (The Sage commtext series ; v. 22)
    Bibliography: p.
    Includes index.
    ISBN 0–8039–3501–3. — ISBN 0–8039–3502–1 (pbk.)
    1. Mass media—Economic aspects.   I. Title.   II. Series.
  P96.E25P53   1989
   338.4'730223—dc2089–35550
  CIP

First Printing, 1989

CONTENTS

For Helena Caroline

1

INTRODUCTION TO THE
STUDY OF MEDIA ECONOMICS

Media economics is concerned with how media operators meet the informational and entertainment wants and needs of audiences, advertisers, and society with available resources. It deals with the factors influencing production of media goods and services and the allocation of those products for consumption. This chapter explores these factors and the development of the principles of the market economy in which media operate.

This book is concerned with the economic aspects of mass media. It is intended to help find answers to such questions as: How could *USA Today* be established when hundreds of daily newspapers have died nationwide? Why have Home Box Office, Showtime, USA Network, the Family Network, and other cable channels significantly diminished broadcast network affiliates' audiences but not as strongly affected independent stations' audiences? Why does the videocassette market bear more resemblance to the book market than the television programming market? Why doesn't raising prices of newspaper subscriptions influence publishers the same way that raising cable television subscription prices affects cable systems? Will producing more record albums increase or decrease a company's financial return?

In order to consider such questions fully, it is necessary to understand the economic milieu in which the media operate. This requires knowledge of the nature of economic study and the development of economic principles and market capitalism. This book is intended to help develop that knowledge by focusing on media in the United States, a western capitalist nation. Although the fundamental principles and concepts can be applied in other settings with different economic systems and industrial structures, the U.S.-based examples presented in this book are not intended to be indicative of media situations in those settings. This chapter is intended to introduce basic elements in the study of economics to help provide a base for specific concepts and issues that will be discussed further in later chapters that relate more directly to media.

Economics is the study of how limited or scarce *resources* are *allocated* to satisfy competing and unlimited *needs* and *wants*, and of the forces that direct and constrain that activity. Scarcity exists because resources are finite, whereas wants tend to be infinite, exceeding available resources.

Economics is the study of the production and consumption of resources and products, as well as the choices made to meet needs and wants. *Production* is the creation of goods and services for consumption. *Consumption* is the use of goods and services or resources to satisfy wants and needs. Individuals and firms are both producers and consumers in that they consume resources and produce goods and services.

In order to consider the ways in which these activities take place and the effects that these activities have, economists have divided the study of economics into two major branches, macroeconomics and microeconomics. *Macroeconomics* studies and analyzes the operation of the economic system as a whole, usually at the national level, to understand its relationship to issues such as economic growth, employment, and inflation. Macroeconomic studies often focus on political economy, that is, the public policies toward the economy, aggregate production and consumption of goods, employment and income, and policies to stimulate or retard growth or promote social welfare.

Microeconomics departs from the large scale and considers the market system in operation, looking at the economic activities of producers and consumers in specific markets. It considers the behavior of individual producers and consumers, as well as of aggregate groups of producers and consumers in those markets.

There is an interplay between macroeconomics and microeconomics. Government actions and policies affect the decisions of producers and consumers, and the performance of various product markets in turn stimulates government action or inaction. The predominant focus of this book will be microeconomic, that is, looking at the activities of consumers and producers in media markets. These activities are influenced by macroeconomic factors, and so these concepts will be introduced as well.

NEEDS AND WANTS

Needs and wants are both public and private. Individuals and societies must make decisions about which needs and wants get satisfied and to what degrees. *Private wants and needs* include subsistence, convenience, and individually determined wants and needs. Subsistence needs include those basic elements necessary for survival, such as food, clothing, and shelter. Human beings are not satisfied with mere subsistence, however. Once those needs are met, they have convenience wants that they seek to satisfy. These include the goods and services that make life easier, more comfortable, and more convenient, such as washing machines, automobiles, and prepared foods. In addition to such wants, individuals usually have psychologically motivated wants, such as fame, belonging, and status, that can be partly satisfied through the acquisition or use of resources.

Each society also has it own wants and needs that leaders attempt to satisfy. These *public wants and needs* include such items as military forces to protect against foreign aggressors, police forces to protect individuals and property from criminals, highways and transportation infrastructures, public education, and social services. Each of these public wants and needs competes with the others for scarce resources, and the public sphere competes with the private sphere for resources as well.

Media organizations function in the economic system to meet both private and public needs and wants. Media serve the wants and needs of four distinct groups: 1) media owners, the individuals or stockholders who own media outlets; 2) audiences, those who view, listen to, or read media content; 3) advertisers, those who purchase time or space to convey messages to audiences; and 4) media employees, those who work for the firms.

In general terms, each of these four constituencies has the following wants and needs: Owners want the preservation of the firm and its assets, high rates of return on their investments, company growth, and increase in value of the firm and, thus, their investment. Audiences want high quality media products and services, at a low cost if the product or service is purchased, and they wish to be able to acquire the media product with ease. Advertisers want access to their targeted audiences, at a low price, and high quality service from media employees. Employees want good compensation, fair and equal treatment, safe and pleasant working conditions, and psychic rewards for their labor. As will be shown later, media, audiences, advertisers, and employees are all involved in both consumption and production.

Media also serve public wants and needs by providing forums in which ideas and issues may be conveyed that are necessary for the maintenance of social order and progress. Public wants for media include multiple stable media outlets, organized use of resources, and content diversity.

ALLOCATION

The resources available to produce goods and services to satisfy private and public needs and wants are scarce, and meeting all the wants is impossible. As a result, choices are made among the wants and available resources to determine which and how many of the wants will be satisfied. This process is called *allocation* of resources.

Allocation involves determining what is produced, how it is produced, and who consumes the products made. Allocation involves three major choices in using available resources: 1) what good should be produced; 2) how should it be produced; and 3) who gets to consume the good or service.

The first issue involves answering the questions of *what* should be produced and made available to meet wants and, secondarily, *how much* should be produced to meet those wants. In the public sector, for example, this decision involves questions about whether government funds should be directed to pay for "Star Wars" or to provide housing for the homeless. In the realm of media, it involves public choices over whether the government should allocate available broadcast frequencies for more local television stations or for mobile telephone communications. In the private sector, this type of decision involves choices of whether a company should make calculators or adding machines, or in media whether a recording firm should use its money to record ten artists or only five, but to produce more of the latter's recordings. It also involves the question of whether the firm should produce the recordings as records, cassettes, compact discs, or a combination of the three products.

The second allocative issue involves *how* the goods are made. That is, who or what will do that work? Will human or machine labor be used? What type of tools and technology will be employed? The issue of where the goods will be made must also be answered. In media these allocative issues are addressed by answering questions such as whether live disc jockeys or automated playback equipment should be used in radio stations, and whether a television program should be filmed in a studio in Hollywood or Toronto.

The third major issue is *who* will consume the goods and services. That is, how will they be distributed among people and industries? The answer to this question is based on the pattern of decision making adopted in a society. Four major allocation patterns are common: 1) *traditional decision making*, in which choices are based on repetition of earlier decisions, socioeconomic or class status, and other factors; 2) *market decision making*, in which the amount of supply and consumer demand determines prices, which in turn influence production and who is able to receive goods and services; 3) *centralized decision making*, in which choices are made by authorities and planning boards; and 4) *mixed decision making*, which combines elements of market and centralized decision making.

Allocation in the United States and most western nations is done by mixed decision making, with a great reliance on the market but some central planning. Most communist nations in Eastern Europe, Asia, and other parts of the world are also using mixed decision making, but with great reliance on central planning and some reliance on the market economy.

DEVELOPMENT AND PRINCIPLES OF THE MARKET ECONOMY

The market economy, that is, a system in which allocative decisions are made on the basis of the economic forces controlling operations of the market, is the primary basis of the capitalist or free enterprise economic system. This system emerged when production and distribution of goods and services moved outside the control of state authorities through the decline of the feudal system. Political and economic systems then developed that led to the accumulation of wealth that could be used for production of additional goods and services. These basic elements were then combined with a concurrent development of technology that increased production and led to a greater division of labor and the general rise of living standards in the eighteenth and nineteenth centuries.

The major political, social, and economic upheaval caused by the transition from feudalism to mercantilism to the market economy was watched with interest during the seventeenth and eighteenth centuries by a number of observers, who attempted to understand and explain the new market-based order that was emerging in England, Germany, and France. Their observations were synthesized and rearticulated in a comprehensive form by Adam Smith in 1776 in *The Wealth of Nations*. Smith argued that the market system's operation was based on several major principles. These include:

1) Competition between different producers and competition between different consumers are the central elements of the system.
2) Consumers and producers have equal strength in the market.
3) Economic self-interest of producers and consumers will be used as a guide in all production and consumption decisions.

4) The market is its own regulator and will operate in an orderly fashion, producing what is needed and wanted by consumers, in the amounts needed and wanted by consumers, at prices consumers are willing to pay and at which producers are willing to sell. The market constantly readjusts to meet changing needs and wants and the demand of consumers of products. (Smith, 1776/1952)

Smith argued that if the market was left alone ("laissez-faire") to operate according to these basic principles, capital would be accumulated that could be used for new production, resulting in growth in the national economy. This would improve the quality of life for all men and women, and society as a whole would be improved. Smith saw this process as inevitable, continuous, and orderly.

A corollary theory of the marketplace of ideas followed, based on the economic marketplace and the argument that an ideal market allowed to operate without constraint would provide the public the opportunity to select from among the most meritorious of the ideas and information offered. In such a system, it was argued, truth would ultimately emerge and the individuals and society would benefit.

As the capitalist market-based system continued to develop during the eighteenth and nineteenth centuries, economists began observing differences between the way it had been described by Smith and others, and the way it actually operated. A number of observers began questioning Smith's view that the marketplace was orderly, and that the results would inevitably, by continuous growth of the economy, improve the quality of life of all members of society. These critics included capitalists such as Robert Owen and members of the nobility such as Henri de Saint-Simon, who believed that the market must be tempered by Christian ethics lest it become an immoral quest for accumulation that impoverished and enslaved workers. Socialists, such as Gracchus Babeuf, William Godwin, and Pierre J. Proudhon, argued that the market system created inequalities that must be eliminated.

David Ricardo, Karl Marx, and other nineteenth-century economists further described the economic mechanisms that created these problems. Marx put forth his views and synthesized others' observations to add additional understanding of how the market system worked. Among the principles he laid out were the following:

1) Consumers' demands for and producers' supplies of goods and services are never perfectly matched. There is a mismatching of production and consumption that creates lag times in responses to demand and misreadings of demand by producers. As a result, there is a regular cyclical expansion and contraction of the economy in what is now called the business cycle.

2) Accumulation of capital leads to the creation of bigger firms that have unequal power over smaller firms. This diminishes competition between producers, creates unequal power between producer and consumer, and thus diminishes or removes the benefits of the market system.

3) The use of machinery instead of human labor permits producers to provide goods and services at lower prices, but at lower profit margins as well. As profit margins decline, weaker firms are unable to survive and are closed or merged with other firms. This diminishes competition and its benefits. (Marx, 1867/1952)

The bases of the development of economic thought are well outlined in such classic works as J. F. Bell's *A History of Economic Thought* (1967), Charles Gide and Charles Rist's *History of Economic Doctrines* (1979), Joseph F. Schumpeter's *Ten Great Economists* (1965), and Lewis H. Haney's *History of Economic Thought* (1949), as well as Robert L. Heilbroner's more popular work, *The Worldly Philosophers* (1980).

The market system problems described by both capitalists and socialists led to the development of large business enterprises throughout the developed world. Concurrently, the idea of *the firm* as a separate economic entity with its own self-interest emerged. Larger firms purchased small firms and merged to create even larger firms. Producers formed trusts and cartels whereby they could control supply of raw materials, production of goods, and price of products. Capitalist nations responded by creating laws supporting the market system that outlawed many anticompetitive actions and the creations of trust and cartels. In the United States the Sherman Antitrust Act of 1890 and the Clayton Antitrust Act of 1914 were enacted to outlaw activities that undermined the system.

The large firms that developed by the latter half of the nineteenth and early twentieth centuries also used their economic power in ways that disadvantaged laborers, did not share the wealth accumulated through the market system as Smith had envisioned, and kept many persons in untenable social conditions. In response, workers organized labor unions, and governments enacted legislation throughout the capitalist world to promote better working and living conditions by regulating job safety, minimum wages, and hours worked, and by providing mechanisms of basic social welfare for workers harmed in depressed periods of market operation.

The basic principles of the market system have remained the same since the early twentieth century, but the changes sparked by government intervention have resulted in mixed economies rather than pure market economies. New theories to explain operations within the broad principles of the market economy have appeared since that time, but these have tended to focus on government activities at the macroeconomic level or on specific elements of microeconomics that develop understanding based on the broad principles outlined above.

MEDIA AND THE MARKETPLACE

Media in the United States are for the most part capitalist ventures, operated by private parties for the purpose of generating profit, and are thus subject to the operational principles of the market system. Even not-for-profit media — such as public broadcasting or organization-operated media — are influenced by the principles of the market system and are thus affected by its operations.

Because these principles affect the operations of media, one needs to understand how they apply to media. It is also necessary to understand the issues that are raised in media operations as individual and aggregate firms produce media goods and services for consumption by individual and aggregate consumers.

Communication firms use scarce resources — electricity, paper, equipment, skilled labor, programming, information — to satisfy their wants to produce media goods and services and gain profit. Consumers use scarce resources — time and money — to satisfy their wants and needs to acquire information and be entertained by media products or to get their message carried in media. Because the resources of producers and consumers are scarce, producers of media goods and services and consumers of media goods and services are constrained in their abilities to meet all the wants and needs they have for media products. Thus, each turns to allocation to determine what and how media products will be produced and how and by whom they will be consumed. Media economics focuses on these basic issues, concentrating on the operations of economic principles in media markets.

Media cannot be considered separately from the economic system in which they operate because the economic forces of the system direct and constrain the choices of those who manage media, just as they do the choices of managers of any other industry. This book is concerned with those forces and how they affect media, and provides a framework for understanding the underpinnings of the economic system affecting media and the specific issues that arise in media economics. The approach is what is called positive, or applied, economics, which concentrates upon what actually happens and can be shown to occur. From time to time allusions will be made to the more theoretical branch of economics, which proposes what might occur under given circumstances or attempts to structure broader operations within a larger framework. This book will not concentrate upon these ideas, however, but upon those that will be most useful to students of media and to media managers in analyzing and making economic decisions.

2

THE CONCEPT AND ROLE OF THE MARKET

The economic behavior of media is impelled and constrained by the characteristics of and influences on media markets. This chapter discusses how markets are defined, how similar and dissimilar media compete, and how different market structures affect that competition and the products available to consumers in the market.

Every industry has different characteristics, but they all participate in markets that can be analyzed using similar concepts. It is important for media personnel to understand these concepts because the nature and structures of markets significantly affect their work. Such knowledge is essential for advertising sales personnel at the Los Angeles *Times* to understand whether they are in the same market as the *Daily News*; it is crucial for the circulation manager of *Atlantic Monthly* to know whether his magazine is competing with *Reader's Digest* for readers; and it is necessary for the programmer at WBZ-TV in Boston to know whether the station is competing with videocassette rentals for its audience and to what degree.

Although there are some similarities, media industries differ from many other industries in terms of the markets in which they operate, the amount and nature of competition in those markets, and their unique concentration and monopoly characteristics. Media serve public interests that have resulted in regulatory control of the structures of some media industries and at the same time media have special constitutional protection in order to carry out their public interest role. This chapter outlines the structure of the good and service markets in which media participate, the nature of the geographical markets in which they operate, and the availability of substitute goods and services within those markets, as well as the effects that these factors have on media operations.

the sellers' *good or service* — the commodity or labor available for trade — the geographical locations of sellers and buyers, and the willingness of the buyers and sellers to engage in trade.

There are many markets for goods and services because the availability of these resources is influenced by geographic areas in which various sellers and buyers are willing and able to conduct their transactions. A *market* consists of sellers that provide the same good or service, or closely substitutable goods or services, to the same group of consumers. The geographic market determines the boundaries in which these sellers offer the same good or service to the same buyers. In economic discussions of markets, it is necessary to define a specific market in which such activity takes place. This is especially true when discussing media markets, because they are somewhat more complex than those of many other industries. Defining a market involves specifying the *good/service markets* involved and *combining* that description with a specific *geographic market* description.

THE MEDIA GOOD/SERVICE MARKET

In economic terms, media industries are unusual because they operate in what is called a *dual product market*. They create one product but participate in two separate good and service markets (Figure 2.1). Performance in each market affects performance in the other.

The first market in which media participate is that for the *good*, the media product. This good (sometimes called the content product) is the information and entertainment packaged and delivered in the form of a printed newspaper, magazine, or book, a radio or television broadcast, cable service, or a film or video production. This product is marketed to media consumers. Performance in this market is measured in a variety of ways. For newspapers and magazines, it is measured by circulation statistics for subscribed and single copy sales circulation or revenue from that circulation. For books and videos, performance is measured by the number of books or videocassettes sold or revenue from those sales. Broadcast performance is measured by audience ratings, and films are judged by tickets sold.

Marketing content to consumers involves attracting their attention to the product so that they will exchange either their time and/or time and money for the product. Not all media require that consumers pay money for the content product, but all consumers must pay with their time, a scarce resource. Daily newspapers, magazines, books, videocassettes, cable television service, and films typically require a purchase by

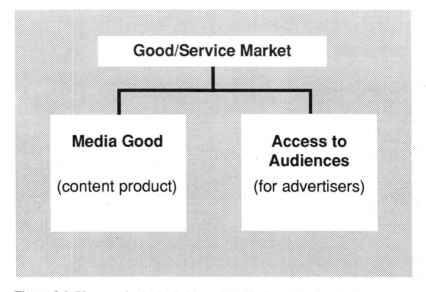

Figure 2.1 Elements in the Definition of Media Good/Service Markets

consumers, but radio and television broadcasters offer their services without charge to consumers.

Differing characteristics of goods affect demand for goods and consumption of goods. A good is considered to be a *private good* if its use by one consumer diminishes its availability to others. A *public good*, however, does not diminish the availability of the good to others. Media are both private and public goods, depending upon their attributes (see Table 2.1). A consumer who purchases a copy of a newspaper diminishes the number of available copies; thus a newspaper is a private good. A consumer who views a television broadcast, however, does not consume it in a fashion that diminishes its availability to other viewers, so it is a public good.

The second market in which many media participate is the advertising market. Although some observers may casually conclude that media sell space or time to purchasers of advertising, a more precise and descriptive explanation is that media sell *access to audiences* to advertisers. The amount charged for bringing readers and viewers into contact with advertisers' messages is more dependent upon the sizes and characteristics of audiences to which access is provided than the sizes or lengths of the advertisements themselves. Not all media participate in this advertising market, however; some rely solely on revenue from sales of the content product and others are funded by contributions. Examples of media that do not participate in the advertising-based

TABLE 2.1 Public and Private Goods in the Media

Medium	Private Good	Public Good
Books	x	
Cable programming		x
Films		x
Magazines	x	
Newspapers	x	
Radio broadcasts		x
Recordings	x	
Television broadcasts		x
Videocassettes	x	

market include public radio and television, adless publications such as *Consumer Reports* and *Mad* magazine, books, and film and video productions. Media that provide access to audiences to advertisers do so in a variety of ways and provide access to subcategories of the advertising market — including local advertising, classified advertising, insert advertising, and national advertising — in varying degrees.

Media, then, participate in the dual markets differently. Some participate in both markets and some participate in only one, and the degree to which they compete in each market differs as well (see Table 2.2).

THE GEOGRAPHIC MARKET

Media units operate in specific geographic markets and are inextricably linked to those markets by the product content and advertising services they provide within those markets. Some media operations compete nationwide, including nationally circulated magazines and newspapers (such as *USA Today*, the *Christian Science Monitor*, and the *Wall Street Journal*), radio, television and cable networks and syndication firms, national magazines, and book, videocassette, and film companies. Most individual units of media, such as individual newspapers, television and radio stations, cable operators, and regional and local magazines, are linked to specific local geographic markets.

The standards and means of determining local geographic markets vary among media industries, based upon inherent differences in the media and ways in which audiences of various media are analyzed. For newspapers, the retail trading zone (RTZ) is the relevant geographic market in most situations because this is the zone in which the primary business for retail and classified advertising lineage and circulation is

TABLE 2.2 Markets in Which Media Participate

Medium	Content Paid	Market Nonpaid	Local Ads	Advertising Class. Ads	Market Inserts	Nat'l Ads
Books	*					
Cable						
networks	(some)	*				*
local service	*		*	+		
Films	*					
Magazines						
local	*	(some)	*	+		
national	*	(some)		+		*
Newspapers						
daily	*		*	*	+	+
weekly	*	(some)	*	+	+	
shoppers		*	*	+	*	
Radio						
networks	*					*
local-comm.		*	*			+
noncommercial		*				
Recordings	*					
Television						
networks	*					*
local-comm.		*	*			+
noncommercial		*				
Videocassettes	*					

* = primary market + = secondary market

conducted. In some situations, the metropolitan area (metro area) may be the appropriate geographic market; in other cases, papers limit their markets to a designated primary market area (PMA).

Television and radio stations operate on electromagnetic frequencies within geographic markets specified by the Federal Communications Commission (FCC). Because of variances in geographic markets defined by the FCC for stations in the same location, the broadcast and advertising industries have developed standardized geographic areas defined by the Arbitron Co. as the Area of Dominant Influence (ADI) or by the A. C. Nielsen Co. as the Designated Market Area (DMA).

The geographic markets of cable television systems are specifically designated within their franchise agreements, but many other local media — including weekly newspapers and local and regional magazines — select and specify their own geographic markets. In some unique situations, the location in which a medium is produced is much smaller than the geographic market in which trade is conducted. This is sometimes the case for newspapers and broadcast stations that domi-

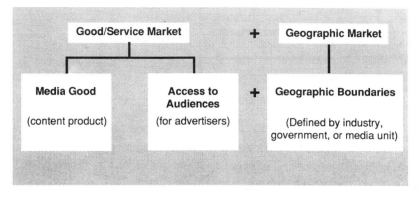

Figure 2.2 Elements in the Definition of Media Good/Service Markets

nate a large portion of a single state, an entire state, or several states, such as the Des Moines *Register*, the Salt Lake City *Tribune*, KFI-AM in Los Angeles, WSM-AM in Memphis, KOA-AM in Denver, and WBBM-AM in Chicago. In such situations a case can be made for expanding the relevant market into a regional market with designated boundaries. When this is done, however, it is often necessary to separate the geographic market for the content product from the geographic market for audience access because they do not always coincide.

Definitions of media markets, then, are created by combining the geographic and good/serve market definitions into a specifically defined market for a specific media unit or portions of its media products (see Figure 2.2).

ISSUES INVOLVING MARKETS

Understanding and defining the concept and role of markets is crucial to managers of media and to those who make public policy because market issues are central to issues of competition and concentration. Many of these issues will be addressed more fully in subsequent chapters, but we must first consider the role of markets in determining whether and how different types of media, and different units of the same medium, compete with each other, and the nature of market structures and market power.

INTERMEDIA COMPETITION

The issue of whether different media compete with each other is inextricably linked to the concept of the market, the dual markets in which media participate, and specific geographic markets in which competition takes place. At the core of this discussion is whether all media products are similar and the degree to which they are *substitutable*, that is, whether media goods and services are interchangeable with each other. To understand the degree of substitutability and, thus, competitiveness among media, one must consider the dual products of media separately and then consider whether the geographical markets for the media are interchangeable as well.

In the broadest sense, all media compete in the content product market by providing information and entertainment. Although media have these content similarities, newspapers, television, radio, magazines, books, films, videocassettes, and other media products serve distinctly different needs and are used in distinctly different ways by audiences. They are not fully interchangeable products any more than football games are interchangeable with ballet performances as leisure time spectator activities.

For audiences, newspapers and magazines serve primarily information and idea functions while broadcast media, film and videocassettes, and cable television serve primarily entertainment functions. Even magazines, which most closely approximate the content provided by newspapers, clearly are not substitutes because of differences in frequency and approach to information. Television, radio, cable, and other media do not provide the range or amounts of information provided by newspapers, and their formats, frequencies, and usage differ.

These differences affect the way in which content is conveyed and the times and formats in which it is available. For instance, television and radio carry news and information, and thus compete with newspapers, but they carry only a limited amount of news and only at specified times. Premium cable television services convey films to audiences, but only after they have appeared in theaters and with a limitation of the visual perspective provided viewers.

Because of content differences, day-to-day substitution of different media as a source of information is limited. Substitution of different media as a source of entertainment is much less limited, however, but is somewhat constrained by the originality and freshness of the material presented. Nevertheless, there appears to be a significant amount of long-term substitution of different media resulting from the development and diffusion of new media technology. McCombs (1972) has shown the willingness of consumers to substitute new media for existing media; this results in significant intermedia competition for audience attention among similar media, such as film, television, and video. Levy and Pitsch, for instance, have shown that audiences are willing to substitute VCRs and cable television (1985). That one medium is not

Production Form	Communicative Form		
	Aural	Visual	Aural & Visual
Inscribed		books magazines newspapers	
Recorded	recordings radio		cable film television video

Figure 2.3 Media Product Characteristics

ing media; this results in significant intermedia competition for audience attention among similar media, such as film, television, and video. Levy and Pitsch, for instance, have shown that audiences are willing to substitute VCRs and cable television (1985). That one medium is not necessarily substitutable for another has been shown by Lacy (1987), whose research reveals that the development and diffusion of radio nationwide had little impact on newspaper competition throughout the country. Similar results were found by Fullerton (1988), who remarked that the diffusion of television induced consumers to make temporary diversions of resources from nonmedia uses to purchase TV sets but that expenditures for media and nonmedia uses returned to their normal pattern immediately thereafter.

The ways in which different media are used and messages internalized by audiences are also affected by the differing communicative and productive characteristics of media (see Figure 2.3). Exposure to aural communications, such as radio broadcasts and sound recordings, usually coincides with other audience activities, and the communications rarely receive the full attention of listeners. This problem is also found with aural-and-visual media, particularly television, video, and cable. Exposure to visual media such as books, magazines, and newspapers is generally voluntary and audiences focus attention on the content to a much greater degree than do users of other media.

The relationships of audiences and different media are not defined merely by use. Important differences also exist in the financial relationships between media and audiences, and these affect the significance placed upon them. Newspaper, magazine, and book readers, as well as and attachment to the product than they do for media products procured at no direct cost, and attend to their content (including advertising) to a greater degree than to those for which no monetary exchange is made.

More substitutability is evident in the market for advertising than in the content product market, as has been argued by Rosse (1980) and Owen (1975), but that interchangeability is limited. Although there are similarities among media that rely upon sales of access to audiences for income, these media are not completely interchangeable because they provide significantly different types of access to audiences. The major reason that media are not fully interchangeable in the advertising market is that their audiences differ widely in terms of product usage patterns as well as in geographic, demographic, and psychographic terms, all of which are key elements in advertisers' choices of media. Variations in the penetration of different media into homes in communities, the length of time that different media receive the attention of audiences, and the types of people using different media create differences in the ways media are utilized by advertisers.

In addition, the various media have unique qualities that make them suitable or unsuitable for various messages (see Table 2.3). For example, the media needs of grocery and department stores, whose managers wish to display their products in ads, are best met by the inherent properties of newspapers. Companies wishing national brand name recognition, such as McDonald's and Procter and Gamble, find television most suitable for conveying their message to meet that need. Firms wishing to provide discount coupons to lure customers use newspaper and magazine advertising, advertising inserts, and mail delivery.

The differences between media products are often not recognized by media personnel, but they have been recognized in legal decisions and public policies regarding media, although there has been some government confusion and disagreement over how to separate the dual products — content and access to audiences — when defining markets. In several cases, courts have ruled that newspapers and broadcasting stations do not operate in the same product markets (see *United States v. Citizen Publishing Co.*, 1968; and *United States v. Times Mirror Co.*, 1967). In 1975, when the FCC promulgated its rule against cross-ownership of broadcasting enterprises and newspapers in the same geographic market, the agency accepted a definition of media markets that blurred the distinction between newspapers and television stations in the advertising market, but specifically excluded other media from evaluations of the availability of diversity in specific geographic markets. The FCC argued: "According to the Department of Justice, newspapers and television stations are in many ways engaged in the same business, namely attracting audiences and selling them to adver-

TABLE 2.3 Strengths and Limitations of Different Media for Advertisers

Medium	Strengths	Weaknesses
Newspapers	intense coverage	short life
	flexibility	hasty reading
	prestige	moderate to poor
	dealer/advertiser	reproduction
	coordination	
Magazines	market selectivity	inflexible area
	long life	coverage and time
	high reproduction	inflexible to copy
	quality	changes
	prestige	low overall market
	extra services	penetration
		wide distribution
Television	mass coverage	fleeting message
	impact	commercial wear-out
	repetition	lack of selectivity
	prestige	high cost
	flexibility	
Radio	audience selectivity	fragmentation
	immediacy	transient quality of
	flexibility	listenership
	mobility	limited sensory input

Source: from *Managing Media Organizations* by John M. Lavine and Daniel B. Wackman, copyright 1987 by Longman. Reprinted with permission.

tisers. . . . Since Justice sees newspaper and television advertising as interchangeable, it would define the product market so as to include newspapers and television stations" (FCC, 1975, para. 35). The FCC also stated, "the Justice Department would only include local television and newspapers in evaluating diversity since in its view these are the only effective competitors for local advertising. Weekly newspapers and other periodicals as well as broadcast signals originating outside the market on this basis should therefore not be counted" (FCC, 1975, para. 48).

The fact that there are differences between media and that these intermedia differences are recognized in law and public policy does not mean there are no similarities among media product markets and that advertiser demand will never be satisfied by substituting one medium for another. However, switching advertising from one medium to another would be based on unusual rather than usual decision making and would take into account a wide variety of factors in a specific market, including the impact of the differences discussed above, the cost for reaching targeting audiences, and differences in the geographic, demographic, and psychographic characteristics of the media audiences in the specific market served by the media. Advertising plans take these differences into account, seeking a mix of media that best serves an advertiser's needs.

Most advertiser decisions about placing advertising in media are predetermined before advertisers seek specific media outlets in which to place the advertising. Because of this preselection of what types of media will receive what percentage of available advertising dollars, most media are not in direct competition and are not seen as direct substitutes by advertisers. It has been noted that

> Advertisers and advertising agencies will usually select the media types within which an advertising campaign will run prior to the negotiation process to purchase time and space. This is because it is believed that there are other more important factors in determining advertising effectiveness than the cost efficiencies between various media outlets. (Busterna, 1988b, p. 41)

If an advertiser determines that a choice exists between two media outlets for the specific advertising message he or she wishes to convey, then an analysis of the geographic market served by the two types of media will be undertaken before determining their substitutability. Although the media may both operate in the same location, their separate geographic markets might preclude finding a substitute. The generally larger markets of broadcast media might extend well beyond a newspaper or cable system operation, but not as far as a regional magazine. These types of considerations, as well as the higher costs of the media serving a larger market, would keep different media from being substitutable for many advertisers.

Some competition among different media in the same geographic market exists, but it is limited. Although all media compete for the attention of audiences in the content product market, each provides varying gratifications to audience members, who tend to use a variety of media rather than a single medium to receive the content products of their choice. Competition for advertising revenue also exists but is significantly limited except among media with similar qualities and content delivery forms. In the same market, television, cable, film, and video compete most directly for audiences. Television and cable compete most directly for advertising dollars, and there is competition for some advertising dollars between newspapers of different frequency.

Despite their differences, advertising-based media compete somewhat in the long run as new media enter the market and alter the types of media available. Expenditures on advertising remain relatively constant as a portion of the national economy (Scripps, 1965), and the addition of new media results not in increased spending but in a reallocation of the existing expenditures among media (McCombs, 1972).

The existence of such intermedia competition over time has been shown in an application of the theory of niche to media. That theory, drawn from the natural sciences, argues that organisms adapt to their environments by developing separate niches from which they compete and coexist with each other in uses of resources. When the theory has been applied to media, increasingly diffuse competition, particularly for national advertising, has been shown to follow shifting use of different media by audiences. Competition was shown to be greatest among media that provide similar types of audience access or message form (Dimmick and Rothenbuhler, 1984).

The breakdown of traditional boundaries between media, such as classified advertising now being carried on cable channels as well as in newspapers, makes it more difficult to define markets that had previously been defined solely by format or production process distinctions. Compaine has argued that "the economists' approach of looking at a specific medium, such as newspapers, is becoming less valid — if it ever was valid — as the technologies of alternative media forms merge with one another" (1985, p. 82).

The answer to this criticism lies in defining good and service markets precisely, and in recognizing that a medium competes in several different good and service markets and that different media compete in such markets to different degrees. Thus, market definitions must include the subcategories of markets in which different media compete.

INTRAMEDIA COMPETITION

Different units of the same medium operating in the same or portions of the same geographic market generally compete with each other to provide content to audiences and access to audiences to advertisers, and can be substituted. This is not to say that there are no differences in the content product or the audience that is accessible to advertisers, because product differentiation and market segmentation result in variance, but that the substitutability of units of the same medium is much greater than that between different media.

If a half dozen commercial television stations compete in the same market — as is the case in many mid-sized markets — the inherent qualities of the content product and type of access afforded advertisers will be substantially similar, although specific programming will differ. As a result, substitution can take place with minimal sacrifice of the attributes that make any one station attractive to viewers or advertisers. If a dozen radio stations exist in the market, however, they will exhibit greater content differences. Normally, they each will have different music and program formats and their audience segmentation and shares of the available audience will be highlighted as they seek advertisers wishing to gain access to the different audiences of each station. Some substitution of stations with different content and audience access products can be made without giving up the attributes that make radio advertising attractive.

The types, sizes, and number of geographic markets for broadcasting stations have been the subject of significant policy debates, but it is now the policy of the FCC to have as many local geographic markets as possible (Noll, Peck, and McGowan, 1973, esp. pp. 97-107). In addition, the FCC is using newly available spectrum and technology to increase the number of potential stations in each of these markets to promote more choices for viewers, listeners, and advertisers.

Units of the same medium that operate from the same location do not necessarily compete directly with each other within the same geographic market, however. It is quite common for RTZs, metro areas, ADIs, and DMAs to include media that compete in only a portion of the market.

This situation is illustrated in Figure 2.4, which shows a metropolitan area that includes three separate cities — Metropolis, Suburbia, and Outskirt City — and an unincorporated area. Three daily newspapers are published within the metro area: the *Daily Times*, which serves the entire metro area and is based in Metropolis; the *Suburbia Gazette*, which is based in Suburbia; and the *Globe*, which is based in Outskirt City. The suburban papers are available to subscribers within the city limits of the towns in which they are published, and single copy sales are available within those cities and some surrounding areas. Thus, their geographic markets are much smaller than that of the metro daily.

In this situation competition is limited. Although both the *Gazette* and *Globe* compete with the *Daily Times* within their primary markets — Suburbia and Outskirt City — they do not compete with the metropolitan paper in the city of Metropolis or the unincorporated suburban area. Neither do the two suburban papers compete with each other. Rosse (1975) has described this style of market structure as *umbrella competition*, in which suburban dailies, weekly papers, and other

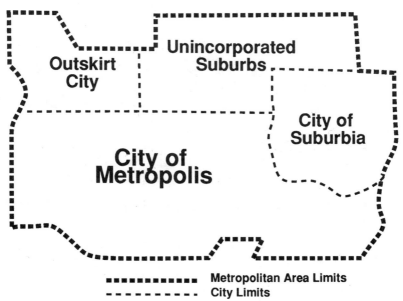

Figure 2.4 Metropolis and Its Metropolitan Area

Rosse (1975) has described this style of market structure as *umbrella competition*, in which suburban dailies, weekly papers, and other publications compete in different layers under the umbrella of a metropolitan daily (see Figure 2.5).

In umbrella competition, the first layer is that of the metropolitan daily newspaper, which reports on and circulates throughout the metro area and sometimes throughout the state or region. In a few situations the first layer includes more than one metropolitan daily, but that situation is found in fewer than two dozen metropolitan areas in the U.S. today. The second layer is that of satellite city dailies. Satellite cities were usually established long before the metropolitan area expanded to include them and have local identities separate from the metropolitan identity and well-established local daily newspapers. The third layer of competition is suburban dailies. These papers operate in metropolitan suburbs created by the growth of the metropolitan area; these metropolitan suburbs have a local identity but closer ties to the major metropolitan city because many residents work, shop, and seek entertainment in the city. The fourth layer of competition includes weekly newspapers and shoppers that circulate in all or part of a suburb or satellite city. Competition for readers and advertisers occurs within and between layers, but great differences in the levels of competition exist.

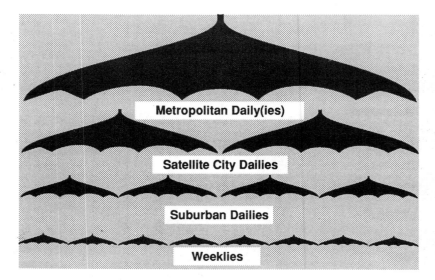

Metropolitan Daily(ies)

Satellite City Dailies

Suburban Dailies

Weeklies

Figure 2.5 Umbrella Competition

cities or metro areas within an ADI or DMA experience more competition from the different layers of competition. A station may identify
strongly with one community and limit its operations to that area,
especially its advertising sales activities. The delineation of a smaller
market is more difficult for broadcasters than for newspapers, however,
because their ability to keep distribution of their content product in a
specific geographic area is limited because broadcast signals do not
stop at city limits, at the boundaries of metro areas, or at RTZs.

For a unit of a medium to be directly substitutable for another, it
must be substantially similar in format and content, garner a similar
audience, and operate in the same geographic market as the other unit
does. In the newspaper industry, for example, a directly substitutable
content and advertising product for a local daily newspaper exists only
when another daily newspaper produced and distributed primarily in
the same geographic market is present. Such situations exist in fewer
than two dozen U.S. cities, including New York, Boston, Chicago, Los
Angeles, and Dallas. Daily newspapers from outside the locality provide some limited substitutability if they are available within the geographic market, but that substitutability is limited. In such cases the
interchangeability involves content originating outside the local area,
such as state, national, and international news, features, and national
advertising. Papers from separate geographical markets differ substan-

tially in terms of the provision of local information and advertising, however. Local daily newspapers can be substituted in a limited way by weekly or other nondaily papers that also provide local, but not national and international, information. In cases where a local daily exists, however, it is rare for consumers to substitute the nondaily as an information source. Instead, it is usually used as a supplementary source of information. Advertisers, however, find that nondailies provide some substitutability. This is particularly true of advertisers who produce inserts and who may be willing in certain circumstances to sacrifice access to the daily paid-newspaper reader for access to a larger audience provided by a free circulation total-market-coverage paper.

Competition among units of broadcast media is far greater than that existing for newspapers. Because of the existence of multiple stations, many with overlapping audiences, a greater degree of substitutability exists among television stations or radio stations for advertisers. Some similar situations exist in the magazine industry, but the audiences tend to be segmented to a much greater degree and appeal to specific advertisers.

Intramedia competition in broadcast television is also influenced by the assignment of frequency and affiliation with programming networks. Levin (1980) has shown that stations with VHF frequencies and those with network affiliations have competitive advantages over stations assigned to UHF frequencies and those not affiliated with the major networks.

MARKET STRUCTURES AND MARKET POWER

The number of producers in a given market is important because it is an indication of the market power that firms possess and their ability to control and influence the economic operations in that market. The industrial organization model provides a method for analyzing markets based on four major market structures: perfect competition, monopolistic competition, oligopoly, and monopoly (see Figure 2.6).

The model states that the structure of a market is dependent upon a variety of factors, including the number of buyers and sellers present, differences in their product, and barriers to the entry of new competitors in the market.

Perfect competition exists when there are many sellers of a good or service that is not differentiated and no firm(s) dominate(s) the market. In such a situation the economic forces operate freely.

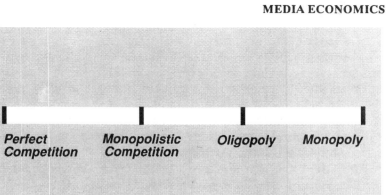

Figure 2.6 The Market Power Continuum

Monopolistic competition exists when there are a number of sellers of similar goods or services, but the products are differentiated and each product is available only from the firm that produces it.

If there are only a few sellers in a market but some competition exists for their products, either homogeneous or differentiated, the market structure is described as *oligopoly*. In such a situation, a greater degree of control over the economic forces exists than in the perfectly competitive or monopolistically competitive situations.

Monopoly market structures are characterized by situations in which a single seller of a product exists in the market and has great control over the economic functions of the market.

Determining which structure fits a given media market involves defining a specific market, analyzing the number of firms within it, and assessing their control over the economic functions to determine the market's location on the market power continuum. If one considers the average markets in which major media industries operate nationally, the industries fall upon the continuum shown in Figure 2.7.

That cable television should be a monopoly is not surprising because it operates somewhat similarly to a utility. Cable systems generally have a monopoly franchise within their areas of operation; that is, they are granted the exclusive right to deliver cable service to a town, city, or metropolitan area. Newspapers tend to operate between oligopoly and monopoly on the market power continuum because the number of newspapers published or available in a given geographic market is limited. The market for television programming, which once was an oligopoly and then in monopolistic competition, has in recent years moved closer to the competitive end of the spectrum because of the expansion of outlets for programming through syndication and cable television channels. No media industries operate in a perfectly com-

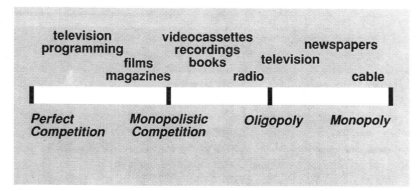

Figure 2.7 Media Industries on the Market Power Continuum

moved closer to the competitive end of the spectrum because of the expansion of outlets for programming through syndication and cable television channels. No media industries operate in a perfectly competitive situation because most media differentiate themselves and try to segment their audiences. The magazine industry exhibits the most competitiveness, but is clearly operating in the monopolistic competition market structure.

Studies applying the industrial organization model to media markets are beginning to appear, including an explanation and application of the model to newspapers by Busterna (1988b) and an examination of barrier to entry into various markets by Wirth (1986), which found barriers higher for the newspaper industry than for broadcasting industries.

Related to determination of market structure is the idea of market concentration. Economic concentration in specific markets provides an indicator of the ability of the marketplace for goods and services to operate efficiently. In economic terms, *concentration* is a measure of the degree to which the largest companies control production, employment, or other indicators of size in an industry in a market. In media industries the degree of concentration in the content product market is calculated using circulation or ratings information. Concentration in the advertising market may be measured in terms of advertising linage or time, or by using revenue figures that are a better measure.

Concentration is measured by observing within specified markets the ratio of total sales or assets of the top companies to the total sales or assets of the industry as a whole. Commonly used measures include the ratio of the top four or eight firms to all firms. Traditional thresholds for concern that concentration is leading to oligopolistic or monopolistic activities that will harm the economic marketplace have been when the top four firms control more than 50 percent of a market or the top eight firms more than 70 percent of a market.

Recent studies of concentration in the daily newspaper industry revealed that local markets are highly concentrated and that even the most competitive markets are well above the levels at which monopolistic behavior is problematic (Picard, 1988a), and these studies have argued that economic pressures in local markets, combined with poor public policies for newspapers, have promoted market concentration and monopoly (Picard, Winter, McCombs, and Lacy, 1988). The television programming and syndication markets have been shown to be concentrated (Owen, Beebe, and Manning, 1974). Chan-Olmsted and Litman (1988) have shown that the cable system market is unconcentrated, but that horizontal and vertical integration are giving great power to a few firms. Other evidence indicates that the book publishing and film distribution markets are concentrated.

A related area of concern, *concentration of ownership*, considers the amount of an industry controlled by individual firms. This type of concentration is usually considered only in aggregate, national terms rather than in relation to specific local geographic markets. Important contributions to this area of inquiry have been made by Baer, Geller, Grundfest, and Possner (1974), Bagdikian (1987), and Compaine (1979), whose data reveal information such as that the four largest newspaper firms control about one quarter of newspaper circulation and that 20 companies receive half of all magazine revenues. This type of information has important implications in terms of diversity of information available to the public and the ability of media to serve the functions ascribed to them in a democratic society. In the economic approach with which this book is concerned, concentration of ownership is considered significant in terms of its concurrent concentration of specific geographical and product markets and the limitations on the market forces that accompany such concentration.

3

CONSUMER CHOICES AND MARKET RESPONSES

Consumption decisions of media audiences and advertisers are influenced by economic choices. This chapter reviews the factors that determine these choices and how they can be measured. Issues such as the value and satisfaction of consuming media products and how prices affect these choices are explored using the concepts of utility, indifference, and demand.

Because we are concerned with how audiences and advertisers choose and use media, and the amount of different media products and services that these audiences and advertisers consume, understanding the activities of consumers in markets is crucial. The choices made by consumers to subscribe to one magazine over another, to watch a videocassette movie rather than broadcast television, or to advertise in a daily newspaper rather than on television are dependent upon the value of the media commodities and services to consumers.

Knowledgeable media managers make decisions based on their understanding of consumers' preferences and willingness to buy, and the value of media to audiences and advertisers. The same forces that affect media consumers also affect media managers when they consider purchases of their own. When the publisher of the Kansas City *Star* considers whether to raise circulation prices and what effect it might have on newspaper sales, when executives of Cablevision of Baton Rouge decide whether to place 9, 12, or 15 channels in the basic cable subscription package, and when the general manager of KGO-TV in San Francisco decides whether to replace a microwave truck with a mobile satellite unit, the choices are based on economic considerations of value and utility.

Value is a measure of the worth of a good or service, indicated by its ability to command money or other goods in exchange for the good or service in the market. The amount of value represents the importance placed on the good or service by consumers. The value is not intrinsic to the good or service but is rather imparted to the good or service by consumers' perceptions of the degree to which their wants and needs

Utility	Indifference
	Total utility is a function of quantities of various goods consumed.
	Consumers select goods to maximize utility within budget available.
Utility is measured on a *cardinal* scale.	Utility is measured on an *ordinal* scale expressing preferences.
Marginal utility of each additional unit of a good/service declines.	Marginal rate of substitution diminishes at any given level of utility.

Figure 3.1 Assumptions of the Approaches

are satisfied by it. As a result, the value of any good or service fluctuates and changes over time.

Value is thus linked to intangible consumer satisfaction, which economists call *utility*. Consumers maximize their utility when making choices in the market and using their resources to acquire commodities and services. Two basic approaches are used in exploring consumer choices and the satisfactions achieved in making selections among goods and services. These consumer choice models are called the *basic utility model* and the *indifference model*. Although both approaches are based on the assumptions that consumers' satisfactions are based on the amount of goods consumed and that consumers maximize their satisfaction by balancing the goods and services they consume with the resources available to them, the models differ regarding how the satisfaction should be measured and how decisions are made by consumers (see Figure 3.1).

The utility approach uses cardinal measurements, assuming that the satisfaction obtained by consumers can be measured using a ratio scale measurement. Such measures have a true zero and a standard interval between the values. Thus a utility measurement of 100 is twice as large as a utility measurement of 50.

The indifference curve approach, however, assumes that no one can truly measure utility but can only gain a relative ranking of that satisfaction. This view is based on the idea that consumer choices cannot be considered only as choices of whether to consume a product and how much of that product to consume, but as choices involving multiple products and differing amounts of consumption of each. The indif-

TABLE 3.1

Activity	Utils
Reading a book	35
Watching a television show	78
Listening to the radio	45
Going out to a movie	86
Staying in and watching the same movie on a VCR	47
Listening to an audio recording	51
Reading a magazine	42
Talking to a friend on a telephone	89
Reading a letter	92

ference curve approach uses ordinal measurement on the assumption that consumer utility has no true zero and that the intervals between values may vary and are not additive. As a result, a consumer with an ordinal utility of 100 can be said to have more satisfaction than a consumer with an ordinal utility of 50, but this does not necessarily mean that the person is twice as satisfied. Thus the indifference approach provides a relative ranking of utility. It concentrates on the satisfaction, or utilities, that consumption of a product brings consumers and can thus give an answer to the question of how much satisfaction is obtained by consumers who use different media.

THE UTILITY APPROACH

In considering and analyzing the abstract concept of utility, economists use a measure of each unit of consumer satisfaction that is called a *util*. This unit of measurement is used under the utility approach to study consumer choices to establish indicators of cardinal utility and marginal utility.

Cardinal utility assigns util value based on some numerically measurable factor. In studying media use we could assign cardinal utility based on average amounts of time devoted to different media daily or weekly. Or, using a survey of the public nationwide, we might determine that listed communication activities have the average utils shown in Table 3.1.

Cardinal utility thus provides a measure of the satisfaction brought consumers by goods and services. But it does not provide an indicator of whether having more of those goods or services brings more pleasure. That function is calculated by what is called *marginal utility*,

TABLE 3.2

Number of Channels	Total Utility (Utils)	Marginal Utility (Utils)
1	100	100
2	185	85
3	255	70
4	310	55
5	350	40

a measure of the additional satisfaction of having more units of a commodity. Marginal utility thus indicates the increments of satisfaction provided by consumption. Thus it answers questions such as "If listening to an audio recording brings you 51 utils, will listening to two audio recordings bring you 102 utils? Or somewhere between 51 and 102?"

Calculations of marginal utility are made by subtracting the total utility obtained before adding the additional unit from the total utility obtained including that unit. Marginal utility can also be calculated by dividing the change in total utility by the change in number of units consumed:

$$MU = \frac{\text{Change in total utility}}{\text{Change in units consumed}}$$

Using such a calculation can answer the question "What is the marginal utility of having more than one television channel available?" Such a question is, of course, crucial to someone considering starting a new television station in a market, or to understanding why most cable subscribers choose only basic cable services.

If we determine that having one channel brings viewers 100 utils of satisfaction, having two channels brings 185 utils, having three channels creates 255 utils, and so forth, we calculate marginal utility as shown in Table 3.2.

This reveals that the marginal utility (satisfaction) of having access to each new television channel diminishes as the number of available channels rises. It is possible for marginal utility to increase in the short run, but in the long run, marginal utility diminishes as each new unit of the good or service is added.

Another way of observing this diminishing marginal utility is to view it graphically, showing utils obtained by each new channel as shown in Figure 3.2.

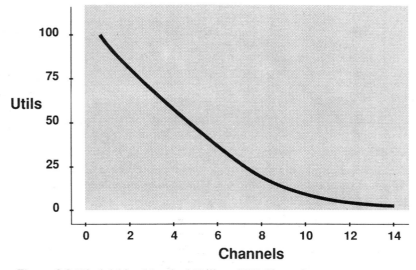

Figure 3.2 Diminishing Marginal Utility of TV Channels

Because of this phenomenon most cable TV viewers are content with access to fewer than two dozen channels rather than increasing their access to as many as the 120 channels that some television sets will accommodate. For the same reason, magazine readers choose only a few of the thousands of titles available nationwide.

UTILITY AND PRICE

Utility thus provides a measure of what worth goods and services have to consumers, that is, a means of establishing value. It must be noted, however, that utility and the price of a good or service are not directly correlated. Water, for instance, is a necessity and has great utility in its satisfaction of wants and needs, but the normal price of water is lower than the normal price of diamonds. This would change, of course, if a person were lost in the desert and the utils of having water overcame the utils of having a diamond. The price of goods and services is determined not only by utility but by the labor necessary to produce commodities and services and other costs associated with the production. And price is also determined by diminishing utility for multiple units of a commodity or service, which is one reason why many products are available in multipacks at a price significantly less than the cost for the units of the product separately.

TABLE 3.3

	Marginal Utility (Utils)	Price	Marginal Utility Per Dollar
Seeing film today	86	$5.00	17.2
Seeing film on bargain night	86	$2.00	43

When making choices in the market, consumers consider both utility and price. For example, if you really wish to see a new hit movie you can go today and pay $5 to see the film or you can wait until bargain night when you can see the same film for $2. When you choose to wait until the less desirable night and pay the lower price, you have decided that the extra cost of going today is not worth it. In analyzing the decision, we can combine utility and price to yield a measure of marginal utility per dollar. Assuming that the marginal utility of viewing the film is 86 utils, we can make the calculation as shown in Table 3.3.

This example reveals that the decision is one of rational choice. The marginal utility per dollar of seeing the film on bargain night (43) is two and one half times that of seeing the film today (17.2).

This example, however, assumes that the marginal utility of seeing the film today or on another day is the same. But this may not always be the case. Suppose that seeing the film today is part of a date with someone or an evening with friends. Such factors might induce you to pay the higher price by raising the marginal utility of seeing the film today through the additional utils associated with these additional factors.

The allocative decisions made in life are rarely as simple as choosing between two alternatives, however. In fact, consumers make thousands of decisions among goods and services. In doing so they seek to maximize their satisfaction. Such maximizing behavior occurs when consumers spend more on goods and services that bring more marginal utility per dollar and less on goods and services that bring less marginal utility per dollar. This is why consumers are willing to spend more of their income on food, clothing, and housing than on purchasing media products. The marginal utility per dollar of satisfying the basic needs far exceeds the marginal utility per dollar of satisfying the wants and needs for information and entertainment.

Although consumption creates utility, this satisfaction is also created by nonconsumption or by saving resources until a later time.

TABLE 3.4

	Marginal Utility of Consuming Now	Interest Rate	Price of Consumption Now	Marginal Utility per Dollar
Example 1:				
paper A	150	7%	535,000	.00029
paper B	100	7%	535,000	.00019
Example 2:				
paper A	150	10%	550,000	.00027
paper B	100	10%	550,000	.00018

Individuals and firms save resources for future use or to accumulate wealth. In determining the marginal utility of such savings, one must take into account changing values for commodities held and interest rates or investment dividends that add to the value of money saved and invested.

Just as marginal utility and price combine to help determine *what* is consumed at present, the two are combined to determine *whether* to consume at present or save for future consumption. For example, assume that two newspaper companies are planning to purchase new printing presses and that they can acquire the presses immediately or sign agreements to acquire and pay for the presses next year. The price for the presses is $500,000. If the papers buy the presses immediately, the cost of consumption will be $500,000 plus the *opportunity cost* of buying now instead of later. In this case the opportunity cost, that is, the cost of the best foregone alternative, is one year's interest that will be lost because the money is not left in the bank. Whether newspaper companies A and B decide to purchase now or to delay purchase for a year will be decided based on the different marginal utilities per dollar for the companies.

Let us consider two different examples in which this might occur. In one example, the interest rate for the money held in the bank is 7 percent. In the second example, the interest rate is 10 percent. In both examples, paper A gains the most satisfaction from purchasing the press immediately. This could be because the current press needs immediate replacement or because the purchase is part of a modernization program that is raising morale and improving the image of the company. As a result of the additional utility of purchasing now, the paper will gain more satisfaction per dollar by making the purchase immediately than will paper B (see Table 3.4). Notice, however, that the

TABLE 3.5

	Marginal Utility of Consuming Now	Interest/ Inflation Rates	Price of Consumption Now	Marginal Utility per Dollar
Example 1:				
paper A	150	7/10%	465,000	.00032
paper B	100	7/10%	465,000	.00022
Example 2:				
paper A	150	10/10%	500,000	.00030
paper B	100	10/10%	500,000	.00020

marginal utility of making the purchase immediately diminishes for both papers in example 2. This occurs because the higher rate increases the interest lost through purchasing now, thus increasing the cost of making the purchase immediately, thus lowering the marginal utility per dollar.

The decision to consume or to save is also influenced by changes in prices. If inflation occurs, goods and services cost more and may reduce any advantage of saving resources for future use. Drawing from the above examples, assume that a purchase of the press today will cost $500,000 but because of 10 percent inflation the cost will be $550,000 next year. Thus the price of consuming now is $50,000 less than it would be after waiting a year, which alters the marginal utility per dollar. In both examples, paper A's marginal utility per dollar is higher for purchasing now than is newspaper B's (see Table 3.5).

Paper A still has greater marginal utility for making the purchase immediately than has paper B, but because its money will be worth less a year from now due to inflation, the marginal utility per dollar of making the purchase now increases for both papers.

THE INDIFFERENCE APPROACH

Although agreeing with the basic assumptions about how consumers behave and that consumer satisfaction can be measured using utils, some economists believe that the utility approach does not approximate reality as well as it should because consumers are rarely faced with merely a choice of whether to consume only one type of good or service, but instead face choices among many types of goods and services. This is particularly true in choices among media products and between media products and those of other industries. The indifference approach argues that every consumer has a different set of preferences that assigns utility to goods and services and to different quantities of those goods and services. These preferences can be ranked by consumers, and economists can study them using ordinal utility.

Ordinal utility is based on the assignment of util value based on rank ordering of consumer preference. An example of creating ordinal utility occurs if one orders by rank the following communication activities in terms of the satisfaction they provide you on a scale of 1 to 100. The numerical value then represents the number of utils of satisfaction each provides.

Reading a book
Watching television
Listening to the radio
Going out to a movie
Staying in and watching the same movie on a VCR
Listening to an audio recording
Reading a magazine
Talking to a friend on a telephone
Reading a letter

If talking to a friend on the telephone receives the score 100 and going to a movie receives the score 80, each activity is worth 100 and 80 utils, respectively, and talking on the phone can be said to provide more satisfaction than going to a movie does.

Indifference, then, uses the idea of consumers maximizing utility by considering what must happen when choices are made involving more than one consumption. Consumers always seek maximum satisfaction and will accept balanced consumption of different amounts of different products to achieve total maximum utility. Indifference is a measure of the point at which the preference between different quantities of different goods and services disappears because the level of satisfaction (utility) is the same for the two.

Assume that you have enough money to purchase 10 tickets to performances at a movie festival as well as coupons for 10 video-cassette rentals. If you purchase both, you have the total satisfaction associated with example 1 below (see Table 3.6). But if you are able to purchase only 8 movie tickets, how many more video rentals would be needed to reach that same level of satisfaction? The answer, of course, depends on how much you will enjoy going to the movie festival

TABLE 3.6

	Movie Tickets	Video Rentals
Example 1	10	10
Example 2	8	12
Example 3	4	20
Example 4	2	25

presentations compared to how much you will enjoy viewing the videos. If you will enjoy each equally, you might find that 2 extra video coupons would make up for the lack of the 2 movie tickets, as shown in example 2. In other words, you are indifferent as to whether you have 10 of each or 8 movie tickets and 12 video rentals.

But what if you could acquire tickets to only a few of the movie festival performances? How many video rentals would it take to achieve the same level of satisfaction? In such a situation, illustrated in examples 3 and 4, the additional rentals of videos provide less and less satisfaction and you need more videos to make up for your inability to go to the movies. You might require 10 video rentals to make up for the loss of 6 festival tickets or 15 video rentals to make up for the loss of 8 festival tickets. This is the idea of a diminishing marginal rate of substitution. That is, at some point, consumers are less and less willing to accept substitutes because the satisfaction received is lower.

Indifference is plotted on what are called indifference curves to provide a better view of the relationships between the satisfaction achieved by different quantities of goods and services. The indifference curve for the above example is seen in Figure 3.3.

This figure illustrates that as the quantity of the one good decreases, the quantity of the other must be increased to achieve the same satisfaction. The shape of an indifference curve is thus determined by the substitutability of goods or services involved. If, however, perfect substitutes were involved, a straight downward line would appear on the graph. If no substitution were possible, a curve of right angles would occur (see Figures 3.4A and 3.4B).

CONSUMER DEMAND

Consumer demand for goods and services is affected by their utility to consumers and the price at which the goods and services are available. *Demand* is a measure of the quantity of goods and services that

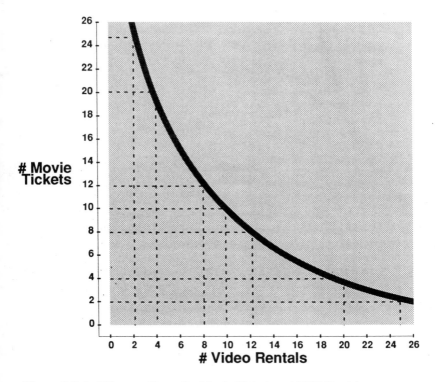

Figure 3.3 Indifference Curve for Movie Tickets and VCR Rentals

consumers are willing to purchase at a given price. Thus, demand is dependent upon the willingness and ability of buyers to pay particular prices for goods and services.

Using the concept of demand, we can estimate what will happen to the number of copies of a magazine sold if we raise the cover price from $1.75 to $2.50 per copy, or how many minutes of advertising we will sell if we raise the price of ads on a TV station from $2,000 to $3,500 per minute. This interplay between price and amount of a good or service consumed is illustrated on a demand curve shown in Figure 3.5.

The graph illustrates that consumers will purchase more of a good or service if the price is low than if it is high. As price for the good or service *decreases*, the quantity demanded by consumers *increases*. Conversely, if price *increases*, the quantity demanded *decreases*. This demand curve holds true for both individual consumers and market demand overall, that is, consumers in aggregate.

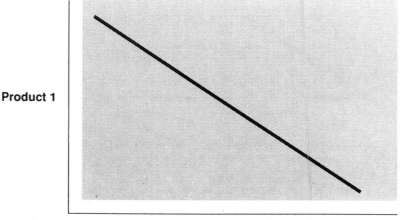

Product 1

Product 2

Figure 3.4A Indifference Curve for Perfect Substitutes

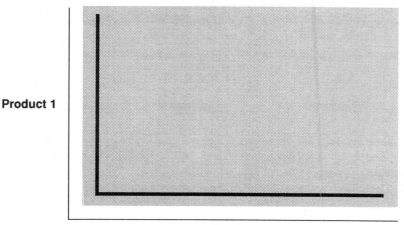

Product 1

Product 2

Figure 3.4B Indifference Curve for Nonsubstitutes

The amount that demand changes when price is changed is called *elasticity of demand.* Demand can be elastic or inelastic, or unit elastic. When it is *elastic,* a change in price is accompanied by a greater change in quantity demanded. Demand is said to be *inelastic* when a change in price is accompanied by no significant change in quantity demanded. If a change in price results in an equal change in quantity, *unit elasticity* exists.

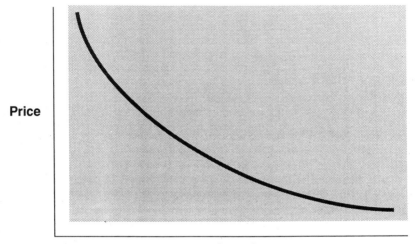

Figure 3.5 A Demand Curve

Elasticity is calculated by dividing the change in quantity by the change in price:

$$\frac{\text{Percent change in quantity}}{\text{Percent change in price}} = \text{Price elasticity of demand}$$

With regard to the elasticity statistic, a negative or positive sign preceding the statistic indicates the direction of demand. This is disregarded in determining elasticity per se. Elasticity is shown if the statistic exceeds 1.0. Unit elasticity is shown if the statistic is 1.0, and stats that are less than 1.0 reveal inelasticity.

Although price is normally the single most important factor influencing demand at any given moment, demand is also influenced by the availability of substitute products and their prices. Over time, a variety of factors influence continuing demand for a good or service, including: changes in consumer income, changes in taste and preference, changes in expectations for the future, and changes in population.

The use of elasticity to measure effects of price on demand can also be applied to substitution of a different product or service when the price of the product or service studied changes. This is called *cross-elasticity of demand.* This concept is useful in discussions of media because it can be used to determine the extent to which different media compete for different portions of media product and service markets.

As a general rule, cross-elasticity increases when there are many good substitutes.

Cross-elasticity is also affected by the amount of a consumer's income required to acquire a good or service. When the proportion of income required to consume a good or service is high, cross-elasticity increases.

ISSUES OF MEDIA UTILITY, VALUE, AND DEMAND

The concepts of utility, value, and consumer demand manifest themselves in major issues when dealing with media: 1) demand for the media product by audiences; 2) demand for access to the audience by advertisers; and 3) demand for units of media available for sale.

Despite the importance of the concepts of utility, value, and demand to media marketing, relatively few studies have been undertaken on the subject. In recent years, utility and value have been indirectly addressed by uses and gratifications studies of media, and some utility indicators can be extrapolated from descriptive audience surveys. Demand studies are more readily available, but their number is limited because most of the information needed is proprietary data held by media companies and industry research firms. Nevertheless, the available data and information provide some important understanding of these issues.

Media Product Demand

The issue of consumer demand for media products is most often considered in terms of media for which audiences pay a fee for acquisition. This includes subscriptions and single sales. Media products that are sold in this manner include newspapers, magazines, films, videos, recordings, and cable service. Although there are similarities among these media, consumer demand for the different products varies.

Demand for newspapers, for instance, is generally inelastic relative to price. That is, a rise in price will not cause a significant decline in consumption. This inelasticity was noted by Landau and Davenport (1959, p. 272) when they found that "the sales price of a newspaper . . . is expressed neither by the interaction between Supply and Demand nor by a relationship to production cost facts. Price determination is purely arbitrary." Several more recent studies have come to similar conclusions. A study of 213 papers over a 25-year period found that demand for daily newspapers by media consumers fluctuated slightly but was inelastic over time (Field, 1978). A similar study of price effects on circulation in 239 papers over a 10-year period also found price inelasticity and found that newspaper circulation rose despite increases in subscription rates and single copy rates (Clark, 1976). A study by Grotta (1977) also concluded that consumer demand for newspapers is inelastic and that only insignificant decreases in circulation will occur at the time prices are raised.

Demand for motion pictures has been shown to be elastic. Pigou (1932) revealed that variations due to price differentials for time of day, whether a film is in exclusive or general distribution, location of screening, and other factors showed that demand is transferable among submarkets for motion pictures.

Demand for cable television subscriptions was a significant concern as cable companies began making extensive investments in operating systems in the 1970s. Predictive studies of demand by Comanor and Mitchell (1971), Park (1970, 1971), and Noll, Peck, and McGowan (1973) based their estimates on available broadcast channels, media use, demographic information, and subscription price estimates. They also argued that the cross-elasticity of demand between network television and pay television (cable) would result in audience losses as high as 50 percent in markets with one and two network-affiliated stations and declining audiences for broadcast television. Their study provided a useful model for studying the cross-elasticity of demand between television and cable.

Many of the early estimates of cable demand have been supported by recent studies. Ducey, Krugman, and Eckrich (1983) have shown that there is a difference in demand for basic cable service and for pay/premium cable service; this difference has resulted in basic service reaching about 50 percent of U.S. households, but pay/premium service reaching only about 25 percent. Bloch and Wirth (1984) showed that demand for both pay and basic cable services is affected by price, household demographics, and programming quality. Childers and Krugman (1987) revealed the direct competition between pay-per-view cable programming, other cable programming, and VCR rentals, which indicates that there should be significant cross-elasticity of demand between those media markets.

In media in which consumers do *not* pay for the product monetarily, issues related to demand still arise, but they tend to focus upon determining the preferences and utility of various media products and programming for audiences. Research by Steiner (1952), Rothenberg (1962), and Owen, Beebe, and Manning (1974) has shown how utility for radio and television programming can be measured as a component for determining consumer demand for certain types of broadcast content.

Highlight 3.1 The Principle of Relative Constancy

"The level of spending on mass media by consumers and advertisers is determined by the general state of the economy. Any change in the level of the economy causes a parallel change in spending on mass media."

(Scripps, 1965)

"What Americans spend on mass communication has not increased with the advent and spread of new media such as radio and television. The money to create two ubiquitous broadasting systems, first radio, later television, seems to have come more from changing media habits and general economic growth than from any fundamental shifts in consumer habits — such as allocating mass media a larger share of personal income. This close relationship between general economic conditions and spending on mass communication media suggests we are dealing with a behavioral principle, the Principle of Relative Constancy. . . . This principle appears to hold under a wide variety of historical conditions and communication technologies."

(McCombs, 1972, pp. 18-19)

Consumers' overall demand for media products appears to be relatively stable. According to the *principle of relative constancy* proposed by McCombs (1972), media spending tends to be constant over time relative to the general performance of the economy and accounts for approximately 3 percent of total consumer spending. Consumer expenditures for media have the same characteristics as expenditures for staples such as housing and clothing. Thus, new media must attract consumer spending from other media spending, rather than attracting spending from other goods and services in the long run.

Advertisers' Demand for Access

Demand for advertiser access to audiences varies, depending on the medium, but few studies of the differences and their importance are available.

Noll et al. (1973) argue that demand for television advertising time is highly elastic for individual advertisers, but that it is less elastic overall. They also note that increasing the number of stations in a market, and thus increasing available advertising time, does not change the quantity of time desired by advertisers. "Demand for viewer minutes is unlikely to be affected by an increase in the number of stations," they argue (p. 36). This occurs because the additional quantity of advertising time supplied to the market by the new stations results in the marginal cost for the advertising time and its price growing closer together, thus reducing the profit each produces for broadcasters.

Picard (1982) revealed that newspapers pay little attention to economics when setting prices for advertising space and that prices are set with more attention paid to industry trends than to consumer demand. Research by Busterna (1987) has shown that there is no cross-elasticity of demand for national advertising between newspapers and television, radio, magazines, newspaper supplements, or outdoor advertising. Norris (1982), after studying the interplay between circulation and advertising in magazines, argued that prices for advertising are based both on actual circulation and estimates of demand elasticity in the advertising market. A study by McGann, Russell, and Russell (1983) found great variability in prices for advertising space in metropolitan editions of national consumer magazines. The absence of price equilibrium suggests that the magazines are setting prices based on consumer demand factors rather than cost or target profit factors.

Demand for Media Units

Several studies of television station transactions have found that demand for stations is affected not just by price but by a variety of market and station characteristic factors that are closely related to the interests of advertisers. Levin (1971, 1975, 1980) found that market size, audience size, network affiliation, age of station, and VHF band frequency affected the demand and price for stations. Levin's findings were matched in a study by Cherington, Hirsch, and Brandwein (1971). Blau, Johnson, and Ksobeich (1976) concurred that the previously identified factors affected demand but found that the price that purchasers were willing to pay for stations was greatly influenced by the annual revenues of the television stations. Bates (1988) explored the impact of federal deregulation efforts on demand for stations and found that it had little impact on demand or on the price of stations.

Factors influencing demand for TV stations have also been found to influence the demand for radio stations. Cheen (1986) identified the market and financial factors contributing to demand for and value of radio stations and noted the important effects of the following on the value of a station: whether a station broadcasts on the AM or FM bands, what its market size is, and what its audience characteristics are.

4

PRODUCER CHOICES AND MARKET RESPONSES

The production decisions of media companies are affected by economic forces. This chapter discusses how production takes place, how inputs are changed into outputs, and how media decide how much of their product to supply. Central to these decisions are the concepts of cost, profit, economies of scale, and diminishing returns.

Those who create products behave rationally in the market and make decisions based both on the costs of goods and the profits they receive from making products. Producers are those individuals who create goods or services for consumers. Production takes many forms, ranging from factory work to housework, from producing feature films to publishing books. All production involves altering or reconfiguring some good or goods for use by others.

Producers make choices based on the costs of production and the financial benefits that result from production and sale of their product or services. These decisions involve the amount, the type, and the price of the goods and services. Thus, executives of Columbia Records consider the additional costs of producing additional copies of an album that has just won a Grammy award in comparison with the additional revenue they may be able to generate. Similarly, Sage Publications weighed the costs of producing this book in hardback and paperback and projections of sales for each in order to determine how many of each to produce. This type of analysis can only be done fully if one understands the nature of the production processes, the use of resources, and the implications of different types of costs for production.

In the production process, *inputs* are transformed into *outputs*. In other words, some resource(s) or factor(s) of production is (are) utilized to produce some product or service or other form of the good used. In media industries, inputs are goods such as information, scripts, newsprint, videotape, and film stock, and services offered by reporters, editors, producers, directors, and performers. Outputs in media are such products as films, records, newspapers, magazines, and broadcasts.

Two main categories are used to describe inputs: fixed inputs and variable inputs. *Fixed inputs* are those which are necessary for production but which cannot be changed to increase or decrease output. In media industries, these include buildings and land, printing presses, transformers, satellite stations, and so forth. *Variable inputs*, however, directly affect the amount of output when their quantity is varied. These include labor, newsprint, plastic for record albums, videotape, and so forth.

Every industry has its unique inputs and production processes required to produce its outputs, and some companies produce similar outputs with different inputs and processes. Most industries require many inputs to produce a single output. The inputs of media industries vary widely because of the variety of production and distribution forms for media goods and services, and the amount and variety of components necessary to produce these products.

HOW MUCH SHOULD BE PRODUCED?

A major issue in production involves the question of how much output a producer should create and what will happen to that output when inputs are increased. This is a crucial issue because producers wish to locate their production levels at points at which their firms operate most efficiently in terms of the inputs required to get their outputs. Although various industries differ in the amount and types of inputs needed, all industries — including media industries — can be considered using an input-output approach, and the analysis of different situations follow similar patterns.

By considering a production situation in which a single input is considered, one can more easily understand the economic issues surrounding inputs. Let us consider the example of a television news director who is considering how many news crews are needed to produce a newscast. The TV crews' labor (the input) is used to produce news packages (the output) and the news director wants to know what number of crews will be most efficient for the station. Obviously, if no crews work, no output is created. Likewise, if the number of crews working increases, the amount of output changes (see Table 4.1).

The *additional output* resulting from the *additional input* of each day of crew labor is called the *marginal physical product* (MPP). This measure provides an indication of what contribution the last unit of

TABLE 4.1 Effect of Input on News Package Output and MPP

Days of Crew Labor Input	Package Output (Total Product)	Marginal Physical Product
0	0	—
1	1	1
2	3	2
3	5.5	2.5
4	7	1.5
5	8.25	1.25
6	9.25	1
7	10	.75
8	10.5	.50
9	10.25	.25
10	10.25	0

input added made to output. In the example in Table 4.1, the size of the marginal product increases at first, to a high of 2.5 with three days of crew labor, but then begins to decline. The area in which marginal physical product increases is known as the area of increasing returns, and the area in which marginal product decreases is known as the area of decreasing returns.

This decline in MPP occurs because of what is known as the *law of diminishing returns.* This law states that at some point the output resulting from each new input begins to decline. This occurs because the increasing amount of input is ultimately used inefficiently. In some situations, it can become so inefficient that MPP not only diminishes but actually becomes negative. Because of the law of diminishing returns, the amount of additional product that can be produced by increasing input can be expected to rise at first but then begin falling. Thus, a producer cannot expect to increase output continually by increasing input.

In the example of the news crews, the MPP begins declining at four days of news crew labor. This inefficiency could occur because some equipment production would need to be shared and the demands of the large number of crews would be expected to cause news crews to wait to use some equipment. This, of course, would diminish the efficiency of the crews and their productivity, and reduce the output benefits of having additional crews.

In situations in which the input and output units are larger and not as easily calculable as those indicated in the example above, the following formula is used:

TABLE 4.2 Effect of Input on News Package Output, MPP, and APP

Days of Crew Labor Input	Package Output (Total Product)	MPP	APP
0	0	—	—
1	1	1	1
2	3	2	1.5
3	5.5	2.5	1.83
4	7	1.5	1.75
5	8.25	1.25	1.65
6	9.25	1	1.54
7	10	.75	1.43
8	10.5	.50	1.31
9	10.25	.25	1.14
10	10.25	0	1.14

$$MPP = \frac{\text{Change in output}}{\text{Change in input}}$$

Another means of determining what happens to output when input is altered is to consider what is called the *average physical product* (APP). This measure is concerned with the average output, rather than the amount of additional output achieved by adding input that is shown by MPP. It averages the contribution of input across all output. Average physical product is calculated as follows:

$$APP = \frac{\text{output}}{\text{input}}$$

Using the example of how additional days of television news crew labor affect the number of news packages produced, we see that APP rises, plateaus, and then declines (see Table 4.2). Thus, as with the marginal physical product, average physical product also has an area in which it increases and decreases due to the law of diminishing returns. But although MPP can decline into a negative situation, the APP will remain positive because it deals not with change but with actual output.

The relationship between total product (the output), MPP, and APP, is shown graphically in Figure 4.1, using the news crew example.

Producers obviously want their combinations of input and output to result in a return of the best possible level of output. To accomplish this goal, producers try to add input as long as increasing returns remain possible and to stop adding input before they reach negative returns. In practice, this usually means not adding more input once diminishing returns are evident.

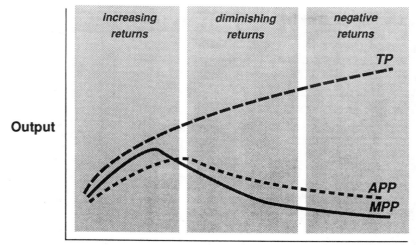

Figure 4.1 Returns on Inputs Showing TP, MPP, and APP

This discussion of input and output has focused on how variations in a single input affect output. As mentioned earlier, however, most outputs require many inputs, ranging from labor to raw materials and supplies. The general principles for understanding the relationships between an input and output are applicable to situations in which multiple inputs are involved. It is, of course, further complicated by the necessity of combining variations in different proportions of specific inputs to achieve the output level desired.

COST, PROFITS, AND PRODUCT SUPPLY

In addition to being affected by changes in input, the *product supply* of a good or service is affected by its production costs and the profitability of producing the product. Producers wish to get the largest quantity of product for the lowest cost as a means of generating a high financial return.

Because of that orientation, a significant amount of attention is paid to understanding the cost of producing various levels of output. The costs of production fall into the categories of monetary and nonmonetary costs. Monetary costs, sometimes called explicit costs, are those for which the company expends money. These include costs for procuring labor, supplies, raw materials, buildings, and equipment. Nonmonetary costs, sometimes called implicit costs, include opportunity costs and the value of uncompensated use of labor or equipment.

The concept of profitability involves two definitions of profit. The first is what are called *normal profits*. Normal profits are the minimal return to inputs that must be available to keep a company or individual producing. Included in this category are nonmonetary costs for one's own labor and psychic rewards for doing the work. The second type of profit, *pure profit*, is the return that exceeds both the monetary and nonmonetary costs. This is the kind of profit most people think of when they consider the term profit in a business sense.

Producers are rational and make decisions based on cost and profitability so that the amount of output produced, the product supply, is based on achieving the lowest possible costs and highest profits.

A primary element in determining product supply is *marginal cost* (MC). Marginal cost is the added production cost for making more output or, conversely, the lowering of costs that occurs when there is a reduction in the output.

This type of analysis involves calculating the costs associated with the two main types of inputs, fixed inputs and variable inputs. The costs associated with fixed inputs are called *fixed costs* and the costs associated with variable inputs are called *variable costs*. Fixed and variable costs can include both monetary and nonmonetary costs. In calculating marginal cost, one combines both fixed and variable costs.

Continuing with the news crew example considered earlier, it might be determined that the fixed costs of maintaining a camera crew are $100 per day and that the variable costs for the crew (their labor) are $300 per day.

Total variable cost (TVC) is then calculated by multiplying the days of labor input by the variable labor cost of $300 per day. *Total cost* (TC) results from adding the fixed cost of $100 per day to the TVC. To calculate marginal cost, one divides the change in total cost by the change in output:

$$MC = \frac{\text{Change in total cost}}{\text{Change in output}}$$

The resulting calculation of marginal cost provides a measure of the cost of gaining one more news package for each day of crew labor (see Table 4.3). If no crew labor is used, the total cost is $100 because the fixed costs exist whether or not any work is done. If one crew is employed for one day to produce one news package, the TC increases to $400 and the marginal cost is $300 ($400 – $100).

TABLE 4.3 Marginal Costs for Additional Input and Output

Days of Crew Labor Input	Package Output	Total Variable Cost	Total Cost	Marginal Cost
0	0	$ 0	$ 100	$ —
1	1	300	400	300
2	3	600	700	150
3	5.5	900	1,000	120
4	7	1,200	1,300	200
5	8.25	1,500	1,600	240
6	9.25	1,800	1,900	300
7	10	2,100	2,200	400
8	10.5	2,400	2,500	600
9	10.75	2,700	2,800	1,200
10	10.75	3,000	3,100	1,200

If two crews are employed, the change in TC, $300 (derived by subtracting $400 from $700), is divided by the change in output, 2 (derived by subtracting 1 from 3), to yield a marginal cost of $150. The MC varies significantly given the different input days and TVCs. It begins moderately high, declines as output begins to increase, and then increases rapidly as output moves upward.

There is an important relationship between marginal cost and the marginal physical product discussed earlier. If they are graphed simultaneously, it becomes quickly apparent that MC reaches its low point at the output level where MPP is at its peak and vice versa (see Figure 4.2). This occurs because when labor is most productive, it is less costly to get another unit of output.

Although marginal cost provides an important indicator about the relationship between alterations in costs that are altered by changes in marginal product, it does not measure the changes in costs overall by such changes. That function is provided by *average costs* measures that indicate the mean costs for each unit of output produced.

There are three measures of average cost: 1) *average fixed costs* (AFC), 2) *average variable costs* (AVC), and 3) *average total costs* (ATC). Each provides an important indicator of the contributions of inputs to costs. Average fixed costs are calculated by dividing total fixed costs by output:

$$ AFC = \frac{Total\ fixed\ costs}{Output} $$

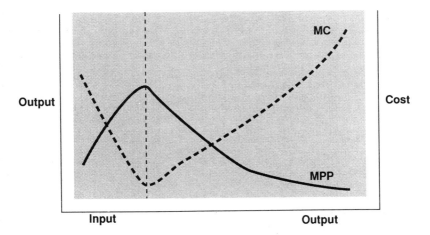

Figure 4.2 Relationship Between Marginal Cost and Marginal Physical Product

Average variable costs are calculated by dividing total variable costs by output:

$$AVC = \frac{Total\,variable\,costs}{Output}$$

And average total costs are calculated by dividing total costs by output:

$$ATC = \frac{Total\,costs}{Output}$$

ATC can also be calculated by adding average fixed costs (AFC) and average variable costs (AVC). Given the television news crew example used before, in which total fixed costs were $100 and total variable costs were $300 per day of crew labor, the three measures of costs across the various examples of input are found in Table 4.4.

Upon examination, it becomes clear that average fixed costs (AFC) *decrease* as the output *increases*. This occurs because the fixed costs are distributed among the increasing output so that each output unit is responsible for only a small portion of the fixed costs. The average variable costs (AVC) also decline as output increases, but they then increase as the inefficiencies of production diminish the return. The average total costs do the same, but ATC reach their lowest point after AVC because of the influence of the AFC decline. Thus, when more of

TABLE 4.4 Average Costs for Output

Days of Crew Labor Input	Package Output	AVC	AFC	ATC
0	0	$ – – –	$ – – –	$– – –
1	1	300.00	100.00	400.00
2	3	200.00	33.33	233.33
3	5.5	163.64	18.18	181.82
4	7	171.43	14.29	185.72
5	8.25	181.82	12.12	193.94
6	9.25	194.60	10.81	205.41
7	10	210.00	10.00	220.00
8	10.5	228.57	9.52	238.09
9	10.75	251.16	9.21	260.37
10	10.75	279.07	9.21	288.28

a product is produced by increasing input, the costs for the additional input decrease for a time but ultimately must rise because return for the additional input diminishes.

There is a relationship between average cost and marginal cost. The marginal cost intersects ATC and AVC at their lowest points. This occurs because the marginal cost pulls the average down to meet it as long as it is below the average, as shown in Figure 4.3.

Average variable cost has a special relationship with average physical product. Average physical product is at its height when the AVC is at its lowest point because the APP gets higher when labor is most productive, and thus the average cost of the unit declines as shown in Figure 4.4.

Producers wish to generate output at the point where both APP and AVC are optimal and the amount produced will be regulated to keep it in that range.

The price set for output by producers is related to the marginal cost. A general rule is that producers will maximize their profit by seeking a level of output at which the marginal cost equals price.

In deciding whether to make extra output to sell, MC and price are considered jointly. If price is higher than MC and MC is rising, producers will increase output until price and MC are equal. If MC goes higher than price, producers lose money on each new unit produced and, thus, cut back output to bring it to the optimal level.

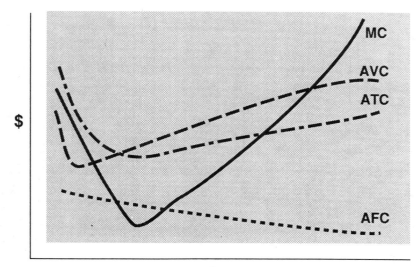

Figure 4.3 Relationship Between Marginal and Average Costs

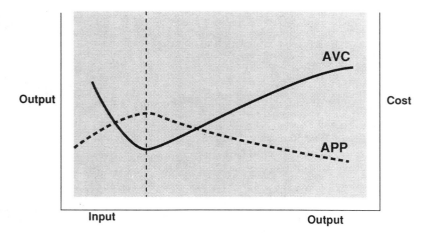

Figure 4.4 Relationship Between AVC and APP

LONG-RUN COSTS

Until this point, the subject of discussion has been what are called *short-run costs*. In the grander scale and over time, one must consider *long-run costs*, in which all inputs are considered variable. Thus fixed variables such as land, buildings, and manufacturing equipment enter the picture. This type of analysis is particularly useful in considering the impact of new products, manufacturing plants, and so forth. In the long run, producers seek a *long-run average cost* (LRAC) in which profit is maximized for the entire operation of the firm. In such a situation, the LRAC is paired with output to determine the most efficient point of operation, and firms try to optimize their profit by operating at that point.

Important to this discussion is the idea of *scale*. Scale economies relate to advantages inherent in the size of a firm or the quantity of output produced. Several important types of scale economies exist: 1) those occurring due to production efficiencies and technology that result in declining average costs, 2) those occurring due to economies of scope, and 3) those occurring due to distribution density.

The scale economies inherent in production efficiencies and technology that result in declining average costs are especially germane to industries with high start-up costs because of capital expenditures for equipment. In such industries, including several media industries, expensive equipment and facilities are necessary whether one produces one unit or many units of output. As the quantity of output increases, the cost for producing each unit — that is, the average cost — drops, and thus large-scale production is more efficient than small-scale production. This advantage of scale is not without end, however, and at some point scale itself introduces inefficiencies, and the advantage disappears.

Economies of scale related to production efficiences of size are sought by developing and maintaining production facilities and equipment of optimal sizes and configurations, and developing and maintaining individual companies at optimal sizes. This concept of economies of scale is easily seen in newspaper production, where the start-up costs, sometimes called first-copy costs, are the same whether one uses the presses to print 1, 2, 50, or 10,000 copies. As the number of copies produced increases, however, the average costs drop rapidly. Related economies of scale are also found in broadcast and cable television, which are also somewhat equipment driven by comparison to other media industries, but the output must be measured in a different manner because there is no tangible product for these public goods. Substitute

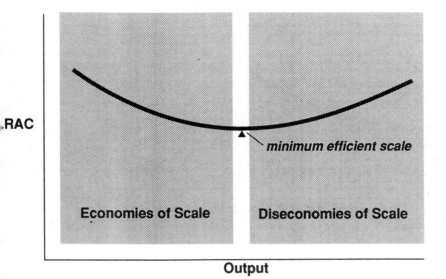

Figure 4.5 LRAC Curve

measures that can be used in analyzing such economies of scale are the amount of programming broadcast or cablecast or viewer or listener time generated.

As illustrated in Figure 4.5, a firm wishes to set its output at a level at which at least the *minimum efficient scale* exists but, preferably, to operate where *economies of scale* exist. At all costs, firms attempt to avoid *diseconomies of scale*.

The LRAC curve is typically a flat U-shaped curve. It begins to decline because production factors, especially technology, bring economies of scale that reduce costs as output quantity increases. In addition, LRAC curves decline when economies of scope exist. Such economies occur when the production of one product lowers the production costs of another product because they share inputs and spread the cost between them. The curve can also be affected by efficiencies from the size of the firm, such as those resulting from bulk purchases of inputs or tax incentives given to locate or keep a firm in a city or state. Further, LRAC curves can decline because of distribution factors known as economies of density, in which a product is distributed densely in a market. Such distribution is cheaper than when distribution is sparse in a market and the costs of reaching customers is higher.

Changes in the curve of any firm can be affected by new tech-nologies that reduce the inputs required to produce a good or services (especially labor-saving equipment), by external factors that increase the costs of inputs, by ineffiencies that enter use of facilities, and by high debt that develops from takeovers of public companies or defenses against takeovers.

Considering production in the long run also allows one to consider the effect of increases in inputs. When these factors are increased, three possible outcomes can occur: 1) a proportionate increase in output — that is, scale is constant; 2) an increase in output, disproportionately low to the increase; or 3) an increase in output, disproportionately high to the increase.

Studying the results of such outcomes, and the long-run costs of operating a firm, provides important insight into the economic situation of producers. Three types of measurements of LRAC are normally encountered. The first is engineering estimates. These are estimates of the LRAC of equipment and facilities that are normally made in the course of considering new technology or plant expansion. The second measurement is based on past costs. This method requires access to proprietary information but can be made within firms. The third mea-surement is a technique called survival analysis, which attempts to identify distinguishing elements between firms that survived and those that failed.

Both short-run and long-run factors affect the supply of a good or service made available. But price still plays an important role. How price affects the quantity of a good or service made available by a producer is illustrated in a supply curve (see Figure 4.6). Product supply will increase if price is high because producers will want to receive the income from the high prices and the pure profits that will presumably accrue. The supply curve applies to both individual pro-ducers and the market supply of all producers as well.

As with demand, the interaction of price and supply is measured using the concept of elasticity. If a change in price results in a greater change in quantity supplied, product supply is said to be elastic. If the change in price results in no significant change in quantity supplied, supply is said to be inelastic. Unit elasticity of supply is shown if there is an equal change in price and product supply. Calculation of elasticity is made as follows:

$$\frac{\text{Percent change in supply}}{\text{Percent change in price}} = \text{Price elasticity of supply}$$

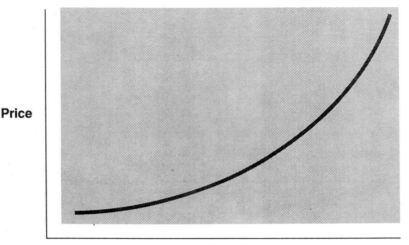

Figure 4.6 Supply Curve

A variety of factors in addition to price can affect supply. These include the price of inputs, price of other substitutable products, changes in producer expectations for the future, changes in technology, and changes in the number of producers.

DISTRIBUTION ECONOMICS

Throughout this chapter, discussion has focused on the production of tangible outputs and the effects of changing input quantity on output and costs. Although this discussion matches the settings in which the newspaper, magazine, recording, and video industries operate, it does not approximate well the setting in which broadcasting, cablecasting, and films most often operate. This occurs because the latter industries create public goods, and their operations do not approximate production economics but can best be considered using distribution economics.

When dealing with public goods, it becomes immediately clear that the cost of production is not affected by the number of users. Production costs of a television show, a radio broadcast, or a feature film remain the same whether many or few individuals comprise their audiences. There are no significant production cost advantages related to scale when the product is a public good being distributed.

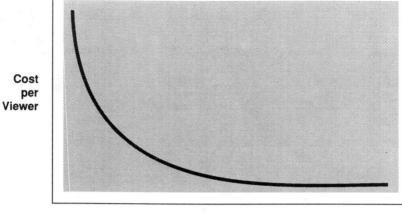

Figure 4.7 Effect of Audience Size on Cost per Viewer

Once a program or production is complete, the costs of getting it to a larger audience by making it available nationally or internationally are small and incremental. This additional cost is all that must be covered by distribution. As a result, great profits are possible in these industries by syndication, networking, and general distribution. By reaching these larger audiences with the product, the cost per viewer drops remarkably (see Figure 4.7).

There are cost differences between programming produced for large audiences and small audiences, but these are inherent in the costs of getting better writers, performers, directors, and technicians to increase the quality of the production. Low-cost productions can, and have, been made available to large audiences without additional production costs. Networks usually increase the production costs of prime-time productions by hiring popular performers and increasing production budgets because the cost will be spread over a large national audience by simultaneous broadcasting through affiliates.

Public goods are also not affected by supply and demand in the same way that private goods are affected. Providing a public good to a consumer does not diminish its availability to others. If a viewer watches a TV broadcast, this action does not keep others from watching. In such a situation, the broadcaster receives income from advertisers and thus seeks profit-maximizing audiences. This generally means the largest possible audience because income increases with audience size (see Figure 4.8).

When dealing with such public goods, setting a price on the product cannot be done with the same type of efficiency found when tangible

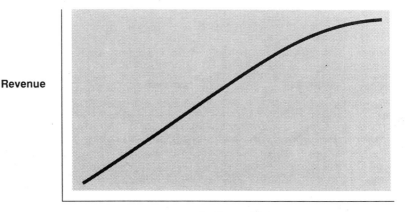

Figure 4.8 Effect of Audience Size on Revenue

private goods are involved. No single price will lead to an efficient equilibrium because any price above zero will exclude some customers, and the potential revenue from them will be lost and cannot be replaced with higher income from other customers. The most efficient price in terms of generating the largest audience is zero, but this removes the incentive for a producer to do anything more than pander to mass tastes.

When audiences begin to pay for public goods, as in the case of cable TV, pay TV, and feature films, the price element begins to affect demand by losing viewers who would watch only if the price were lower. This is particularly true in cablecasting for premium channels.

PRODUCERS MEET CONSUMERS

There is a point at which producers depart from the abstract world of economic projects and enter the concrete and very real world of the marketplace for goods and services. When this occurs, forces promoting or constraining the supply of the good or service come into contact with the forces promoting or constraining the consumer demand for the good and service that were discussed in the last chapter.

Equilibrium is the point at which supply and demand meet and equalize the price and quantity produced. This is the optimal point for consumers and producers (see Figure 4.9). Related to the concept of price and supply is the issue of revenue, that is, income, received from the sale of the output. Determining the impact of revenues on supply decisions is made using the same concepts employed in exploring costs. As a result, on the income side of the ledger one deals with *marginal*

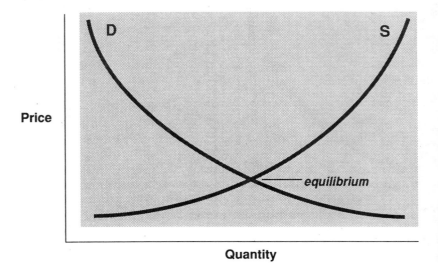

Price

Quantity

Figure 4.9 Supply and Demand

revenue, the additional revenue received from producing each additional unit of output, and *average revenue*, the revenue averaged over all units.

If a competitive situation exists with many small producers, the supply curve for any one producer would allow it to produce as much of the product as possible and continue to receive the same price and additional revenue for each. This is shown in the following example of what happens to revenue for a magazine. As the output increases, both marginal and average revenue stays the same as the price and total price rises linearly (see Table 4.5). If this situation were displayed on a graph, it would appear as Figure 4.10. In reality, the firm could not continue producing into infinity as a means of increasing revenue and profit because at some point the law of diminishing returns will make the costs per unit rise and thus marginal return would diminish into a negative zone.

In most production situations, producers do not operate in perfect competition so the marginal and average revenue curves are not at right angles as in Figure 4.10, but slant or bow downward.

In making production decisions, producers obviously must balance the issues of cost and revenue, and they seek to reach the optimal point where MC and MR intersect, as shown in Figure 4.11. In making production decisions, marginal cost — not average cost — is used in making production decisions.

TABLE 4.5

Output	Price	Marginal Revenue	Total Revenue	Average Revenue
1	$2.50	$2.50	$ 2.50	$2.50
50,000	2.50	2.50	125,000.00	2.50
100,000	2.50	2.50	250,000.00	2.50
250,000	2.50	2.50	625,000.00	2.50
500,000	2.50	2.50	1,250,000.00	2.50

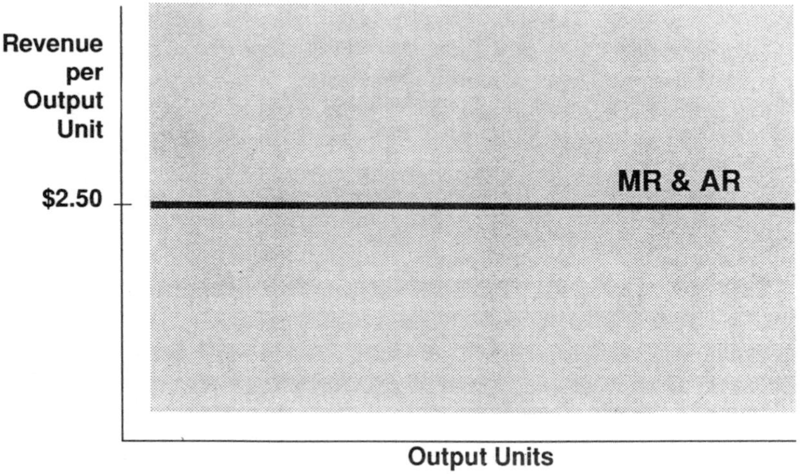

Figure 4.10 Marginal and Average Revenue in Competition

Having established the optimal output level for the price, one can now consider how the firm is doing in terms of profit. In order to do so, average costs and marginal costs are added to the analysis (see Figure 4.12).

Under some circumstances, a producer may deliberately seek to establish disequilibrium. In situations where elasticity of demand exists for a good or service, not all increases in prices will be damaging to a firm, and some may be helpful. An example of this occurs when total revenue increases if prices are raised despite a decrease in the quantity that consumers desire.

A record company, for example, may wholesale 100,000 copies of an album at $4 each, yielding $400,000 in revenue. If the price were raised to $5, the firm would not be expected to receive $500,000 in revenue because some consumers would probably not buy the record

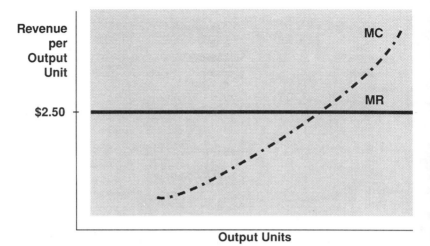

Figure 4.11 Optimal Output

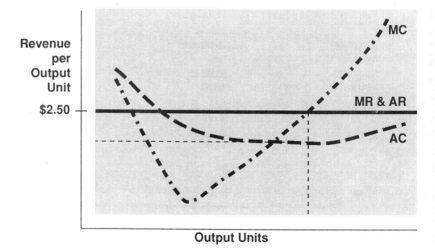

Figure 4.12 The Relation of Revenue to Output and Cost

since a retail price increase would be expected to follow. As a result, the company might sell only 90,000 albums at the $5 wholesale price, yielding $450,000 in revenues. Although the firm sold fewer albums, it is better off because it has an additional $50,000 in revenue.

Thus, firms can attempt to reach a point at which optimal revenue is received by manipulating price and quantity.

ISSUES OF MEDIA PRODUCT SUPPLY

Scholarly and trade literature contains little analysis and discussion of issues related to product supply, such as costs and scale economies. That which exists is generally brief but is noteworthy because of its originality and import.

Levin (1971) has used product supply concepts as a means of analyzing average and marginal costs for using broadcast frequencies and the public policy implications of such costs for expansion of the spectrum. Jane Henry (1985) has provided an analysis of costs in the context of pay TV and revealed that the costs for multichannel microwave distribution service are more favorable than those for direct broadcast satellite service and are competitive with cable television.

Corden (1952-53) used equilibrium analysis to consider the issues of cost, revenue, and output in newspapers. He argued that in considering newspaper economics, quality rather than price is variable for the nonadvertising portion of the newspaper product and that price, quality, and quantity are variable on the advertising product portion.

Economies of scale in cable television have been addressed by Noam (1985a), whose research revealed that few cost advantages occur because of the size of a firm and that economies of scale arise in the packaging and marketing of cable services by large cable systems. Thus, large cable companies have cost advantages when they do more than merely distribute programming through their systems.

Economies of scale in newspaper production have been the focus of Owen (1975, pp. 34-37) and Barry Litman (1988), who significantly explored the issue of long-run average costs and efficiencies and their impact on newspapers. They show that the high first-copy costs are rapidly spread over the printing of additional copies, so that average costs and marginal costs decline. Their work supports important evidence developed by Rosse (1967) that scale economics may be the single most important contributor to concentration and monopoly in newspaper markets.

A few attempts to analyze the effect of economies and diseconomies have been made. Dertouzous and Thorpe (1982) found that economies of scale are not created equally across all sizes of newspapers by the acquisition of new technology, that group ownership does not create significant economies of scale, and that even such economies in newsprint acquisition are not created by group ownership unless accompanied by vertical integration. A survival analysis of the newspaper industry by Norton and Norton (1986) suggests that electronic typesetting technology and offset printing have reduced first-copy costs and lowered the minimum efficient scale. As a result, papers with circulations between 10,000 and 100,000 have survived and grown in terms of market share and number of firms, while firms in the 250,000 to 500,000 circulation range, and those below 5,000 circulation, have been experiencing declining market shares and number of firms.

A study of the survival of new magazines indicates that the scale of the firm is not a factor in survival. The research showed that publications started by leading media companies were much less likely to survive than those started by smaller firms (Husni, 1988). This would indicate that there are few cost advantages in the magazine industry related to size of firm.

Little research on price elasticity of supply has been undertaken, but it has been shown that television programming supply is elastic (Owen et al., 1974, pp. 17-36). Blankenburg (1982) studied how disequilibrium in supply and demand may be used by newspaper firms to increase revenue and profit. In a study of newspaper circulation, he found that some newspapers deliberately manipulate price and circulation into disequilibrium — and lose some circulation — in order to increase total revenue.

5

MONOPOLY AND COMPETITION IN THE MARKET

How media firms behave influences the kinds
and amounts of choices consumers and competitors can make in markets. The behavior of
firms is, in turn, influenced by the structures of
the markets in which they operate. This chapter
explores how product, price, and competition
policies are affected by market structures and
how they influence choices in markets.

The choices that consumers and producers have in the market are
significantly influenced by the *market conduct*, that is, how the market
operates and conducts its exchange. Various markets operate differently because of the structures under which they operate and it is important
to understand the differences in market conduct that are typically found
under different *market structures*.

In precise terms, conduct refers to the policies of a firm or firms
regarding market decisions and policies in dealing with competitors.
Conduct includes 3 major issues: 1) product policies; 2) pricing policies; and 3) responses to competitors. Thus, when Cable News Network
decided to add continuous stock prices to its Headline News channel,
it made a product decision and a competition policy decision to compete with the Financial News Network by providing a similar product.
If the St. Louis *Post-Dispatch* considers raising its single copy price to
50 cents or to stay at the industry standards of 25 and 35 cents, it is
making a price policy decision.

Product policies involve the strategies employed by firms in deciding how to position their product in the market and how the products
will be marketed. Policy decisions in this area involve issues of product
differentiation; product qualities such as durability, size, and colors;
product options; preference building through advertising; and new
product lines. In media, such policies involve decisions about whether
a radio station's format should be top-40, album-oriented rock, classi-
cal, or talk; whether a motion picture should also be released for video
sales; whether a newspaper should be printed as a broadsheet or tab-

loid; and whether a cable network should program classic films or contemporary motion pictures.

Pricing policies involve setting price levels for products and decisions regarding discounting, multiple packaging, and price setting orientation. These orientations include: 1) demand-oriented pricing, in which prices are set solely based upon market forces; 2) target return pricing, in which prices are set based on the amount of pure profit desired in return; 3) competition-oriented pricing, in which prices are based on those charged by competitors; and 4) industry norm pricing, in which prices are based not on market or return issues but on whatever the industry as a whole is charging.

Responses to competitors as a form of market conduct involve decisions as to whether a firm will choose to compete, engage in price competition, or attempt to keep potential competitors out of the market. Policies of competition or noncompetition involve decisions about what product lines to produce, whether prices will be competitive with those of competitors, and whether the firm will advertise heavily for certain products. Such decisions are faced when a daily newspaper considers whether to start a total market coverage free-circulation paper to keep mail advertising services from penetrating a market, when a video manufacturer decides whether to price a video at $79 or $39, and when a magazine company decides whether to use television to advertise its weekly issues.

The issue of responses to competitors in the price area involves whether a firm will engage in price wars with other producers or distributors or whether it will engage in predatory pricing, in which the price of a product is set below its marginal cost as a means of harming a competitor who must likewise lower his costs. Thus losses are forced upon that competitor. A large firm using this tactic is able to absorb losses longer and can force a smaller firm out of business or can force it finally to raise its price at a loss of market share. This tactic is illegal under antitrust law, but it is hard to prove intent and predatory pricing, so some firms use the strategy.

A third policy toward competition involves increasing barriers to entry in the market to discourage potential competitors. One strategy involves observing the price limit — that is, raising the price of one's product as high as one can go without encouraging other companies to enter and gain a share of the market by selling at a lower price. A second strategy is to integrate the firm vertically. When this is done a company acquires other firms that serve other sectors of the industry. For example, a newspaper company might purchase a paper mill and manufacturer or a newspaper distribution firm. The end result is that supplies become less costly to the integrated firm and more costly to

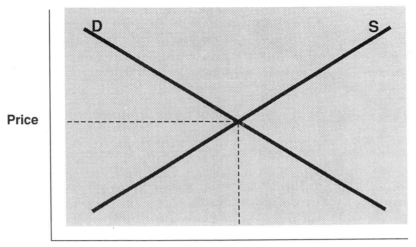

Quantity

Figure 5.1 Demand and Supply Curves Under Perfect Competition

competitors or potential competitors doing business with the firm, so barriers to entry are increased.

MARKET CONDUCT UNDER VARIOUS MARKET STRUCTURES

In a market structure of perfect competition, there are many firms and each has only a small market share. In nearly every case, perfect competition involves undifferentiated, homogeneous products for which buyers have no brand name preferences.

In this type of market, the output by each firm is relatively low, production is labor — rather than capital — intensive, and wages are also low. There is also a tendency toward overcrowding because of the ease of entry.

In such situations price is set by the market alone. The firms are thus called "price takers"; that is, they accept and must conform to the existing market price. As a result, prices are constrained downward. Because producers do not control price, the only production choice that producers have to make is the quantity of output produced. The demand and supply curves under perfect competition are thus straight (see Figure 5.1). The producer accepts the set price level and then decides how much of the quantity demanded the firm will provide or attempt to provide.

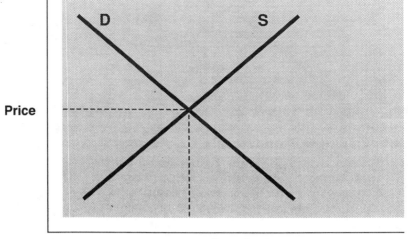

Price

Quantity

Figure 5.2 Demand and Supply Curves Under Perfect Monopoly

No media industries operate under the perfect competition market structure. This is not particularly surprising, however, because few industries operate in perfect competition — including manufacturing industries. The market for agricultural products most approximates perfect competition.

Perfect monopoly, the market structure at the other end of the spectrum, exists when only one firm provides the product, when barriers to entry are high, and when there are no ready substitutes. Typically in such situations, the capital requirements for entry are high, the industry is capital rather than labor intensive, output is high, and wages are high. The supply and demand curve for a perfect monopoly is shown in Figure 5.2.

Under this market structure, prices are set by producers seeking a combination of price and quantity that optimizes their return. The producer is a "price maker"; that is, the firm has great control over price and sets the price it wants. The producer also controls production by increasing quantity produced by adding input until marginal revenue intersects with marginal cost, and optimal levels of price, quantity, and return are achieved (see Figure 5.3).

Producers under perfect monopoly conduct themselves by making three choices: what price to charge; how much to manufacture; and whether to maximize output and revenue. In some cases, producers will

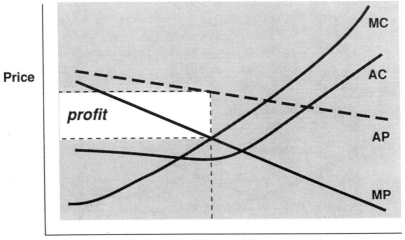

Figure 5.3 Equilibrium Under Perfect Monopoly

choose not to maximize but rather to help communities or serve the public welfare; this, however, is rare in unregulated perfect monopolies.

No media industries operate in perfect monopoly market structures but several come close. Cable television systems are the nearest to perfect monopoly, but perfection is limited because some substitution is possible. If there is only one motion picture theater in town, a near perfect monopoly exists, but some substitution is possible if consumers are willing to give up leaving home and instead view entertainment on a smaller screen. Newspapers have nearly perfect monopolies in some aspects of their product markets if they are the only local newspaper, but some limited substitution is possible.

The oligopoly market structure is found between perfect competition and monopoly but is closer to the monopoly structure. This tends to be a relatively stable structure in which a few firms, typically three to six, share the market, know each other, and watch each other's conduct. Barriers to entry are typically high in oligopoly markets and the products are not typically highly differentiated. The supply and demand curves for oligopoly are shown in Figure 5.4.

In such structures firms tend to have product policies that promote extras and quality differences through heavy advertising and positioning in the market. The firms are able to control price and quantity to a great degree, and decisions on those issues tend to be made interdepen-

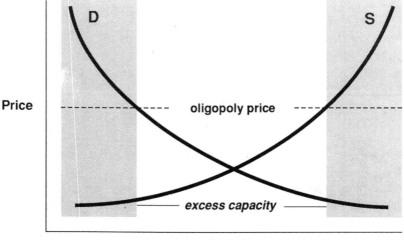

Figure 5.4 Demand and Supply Curves Under Oligopoly

dently with other firms. In other words, the firms have a tendency to cooperate in terms of price and output levels and to set them by watching each other and jointly seeking stability in price and quantity. If one firm cuts prices, others will follow suit, and if one raises them, others will follow. This is called price leadership. Other firms do not have to follow, and some may hold out in the short run to increase market shares slightly. In the long run, however, most producers stick together in oligopoly market structures. A number of media firms operate under oligopoly structures, including many television stations, radio stations, and some categories of magazines.

Monopolistic competition is a structure that lies between perfect competition and oligopoly. In such a situation there are typically a number of firms in the market with some differences in terms of production capabilities and location. There is usually some product differentiation, and the prices and quantity decisions are set both by the market and the firms. The supply and demand curves for monopolistic competition are shown in Figure 5.5

Some price differences are evident in monopolistic competition market structures, but these usually occur within a price range that is determined by competitors' prices. As a result, the actual price is set by the individual firm with an eye on market. In monopolistic competition, a firm's optimal price comes when product quantity yields a marginal cost that equals market price. Monopolistic competition is seen in the motion picture exhibition and magazine publishing industries.

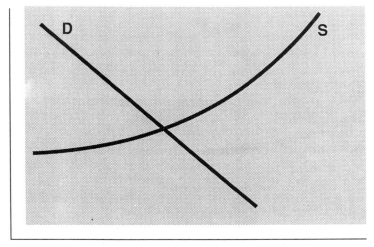

Figure 5.5 Demand and Supply Curves Under Monopolistic Competition

MEDIA CONDUCT ISSUES

How media firms behave in general and how they behave under different market structures is a concern of media economists, and has also been a great concern of media scholars concerned with the important social and political roles ascribed to media. Studies on media conduct have typically concentrated upon product issues (including content), pricing issues, and other management issues. Other studies have explored whether different market structures affect the quality of content or if the structure of one media market affects the structures of adjacent media markets.

Given demand theory and market structure expectations, one would expect consumers to benefit economically from competitive situations and to be harmed by monopolies. One would expect competition to improve the media content and monopoly to harm it. The evidence in this regard is mixed. Owen, Beebe, and Manning (1974) found that network programming and price decisions were influenced by oligopolistic interdependence rather than economic decisions because of time lags between decisions and airing of programming and because advertising prices were also determined prior to knowledge of the actual size of the viewing audiences. This, of course, is a result that fulfills our expectations.

The newspaper industry, however, provides little evidence that market structure has any significant effect on news and editorial content.

Most studies that have compared papers of each type and found few differences have concluded that professional norms and journalistic standards are more important in determining content than economic structure is, and that because of these social factors, the marketplace is not getting diverse ideas and content from different papers.

The development of this line of inquiry can be seen in the work of Bigman (1948), Nixon and Jones (1956), Grotta (1971), Ardoin (1973), Weaver and Mullins (1975), Niebauer (1984), Litman and Bridges (1986), McCombs (1988), Candussi and Winter (1988), and Lacy (1988a and 1988b). Their research has shown that when compared as groups, competing and monopoly papers have not shown important differences in news or editorial content, and local monopoly papers created by the demise of a competitor have been shown generally to continue the news coverage and editorial practices used before the monopoly developed. Papers with joint operating agreements provide news coverage similar to that of papers which compete with each other. Thus, it appears that the presence or absence of competition is again less of a factor in determining content than are professional norms and industry standards.

Chain and nonchain papers resemble each other in the coverage of national and international news and vary little in the type of coverage found on editorial pages, but there is some indication that chains that require the use of their own news services do so at the expense of some local coverage. Not surprisingly, locally owned papers tend to do a better job of covering community controversies as news, but there is evidence that chain-owned papers — perhaps because they are less affected by adverse local reactions — take more editorial positions on local issues than do local papers.

Busterna has significantly explored the effects of cross-ownership of television stations and newspapers in the same market and multiple ownership of television stations on the quality of television news content. He found that neither was related to the size of news staffs of television stations (1978) and that neither was related to local news expenditures (1980), but that cross-ownership was related to more local programming and that multiple station ownership was related to less overall local programming but more local news and public affairs programming (1988d).

Price

Market structure would also be expected to be related to prices charged for products, with media on the monopoly end of the continuum charging more for products than media at the competitive end.

Levin (1971) found some support for this view in his study of the radio industry. Broadcasters operating in monopoly and oligopoly structures used their market power to push advertising prices — and profits — upward until the 1950s, when the number of stations increased and television began creating intermedia competition for audiences. At that point the financial conduct and performance began to move away from what was expected in monopoly situations.

Wirth and Wollert (1984) found that prices charged for television news advertising time were not affected by group ownership of stations, but that cable penetration in markets resulted in lower prices and that higher prices existed in highly concentrated television markets.

Picard (1982) found that the newspaper industry paid little attention to economics and marketing knowledge in making decisions about advertising rates and relied more on hunches than data in making price decisions. This problem leaves newspapers at a disadvantage when dealing with advertisers. In analyzing newspaper market structures, one deals with local daily newspaper monopolies and local daily newspaper competition, which is actually oligopoly.

This pricing behavior of newspapers under competition and monopoly has yielded interesting results. Richard Brown (1967) studied the market behavior of daily newspapers, found differences in the ad rate-setting conduct under different structures, and concluded that the chain-owned papers used target return pricing models and that large papers and papers facing other local daily competitors use profit maximizing models for rate setting. Ferguson (1983) found that competing papers have higher advertising rates than do monopoly papers, a result similar to the finding of Blankenburg (1980) that weekly papers with competition are correlated with slightly higher prices.

Picard (1986), however, found that competing papers had higher actual rates than monopoly papers had, but, when adjusted for circulation, the rates were lower. The results indicated that competing papers raised rates more rapidly than did monopoly papers. High production and distribution costs, lower price resistance, higher salaries in metropolitan areas, and cooperative oligopolistic structures have been suggested as causes for these unexpected results (Picard, 1985c).

Since the 1960s studies have regularly found that newspaper monopolies result in higher advertising rates than do other competing papers of similar size. Grotta (1971) found that when a competitor died, leaving a monopoly, the monopoly newspaper did not pass on the benefits of its economies of scale but instead increased advertising prices, a result replicated in a different study by Charette, Brown-John, Romanow, and Soderlund (1983). Mathewson (1972), Kerton (1973),

Picard (1986), and Candussi and Winter (1988) also found higher advertising rates in monopoly newspapers.

Mixed results have been observed when comparing circulation prices in monopoly and oligopolistic situations, with a tendency toward higher prices in monopoly situations but with the sizes of papers apparently affecting results.

Until the early 1970s, studies of the effects of multiple ownership of newspapers found that chain-owned newspapers were not associated with higher prices. After newspaper groups began to become public companies and began aggressive acquisition strategies, those results changed. Kerton (1973), Bloomfield (1978), Blankenburg (1982, 1983), and Ferguson (1983) have all found that group ownership leads to prices higher than those generated through independent ownership.

Research by Mathewson (1972), Busterna (1978), Ferguson (1983), and Wirth and Wollert (1984) on cross-ownership of different media in the same market has yielded mixed results that lean toward the conclusion that cross-ownership does not affect prices.

Response to Competitors

Few studies have considered the responses that media companies have made to competitors or potential competitors, but there is evidence that many media companies turn to government regulation to raise barriers to entry in electronic media industries. For example, Levin (1971) showed that media companies were responsible for much FCC broadcasting policy that limited competition. Efforts were also made by members of the film and television industry in the 1970s and 1980s to regulate or tax videotape sales. Current efforts are being made by the recording industry to regulate digital audiotape.

Structural Effects

A growing body of literature is concerned with the effects of market structures in one market on the structures of adjacent markets, and most of this research has focused upon the newspaper industry. Lacy (1984), in a study of umbrella competition, found that competition was more intense downward through the layers and was threatening to small dailies in lower layers, but that competition between small dailies and weeklies was not very strong or threatening. A subsequent study found that the umbrella competition model applies well to competition for circulation sales but not for advertising sales (Lacy, 1985).

Niebauer (1984) considered the effects of the monopoly market structure of joint operating agreement newspapers on suburban newspapers, and found no significant evidence that these legalized monopolies have harmed papers in adjacent suburban cities.

The current state of this developing line of research is compiled in an excellent review article by Lacy (1988c).

6

MEDIA PERFORMANCE AND CAPITAL MARKETS

The creation and use of capital are crucial in a market economy. This chapter discusses the processes and issues of capital accumulation, lending, and investing. It also explores how the ownership forms of media firms in their financial performances affect relations with capital markets and the values of media companies.

The performance of media and their ability to gain funds for expansion and growth are critical factors in the management of a media firm and managers need to comprehend the nature and operations of capital markets. It was the existence of capital markets that made it possible for the Media News Corp. to purchase the Houston *Post*, for the Disney company to build new studios in Florida, and for the Little Rock *Gazette* to purchase new printing presses.

The process by which such funds are made available is a relatively recent development in economic history. Throughout recorded history the world's population has created and exchanged goods for consumption, and the leftover wealth created through the exchange was consumed in the creation of individual and national palaces, monuments, and cathedrals. Capitalism developed, however, when the proceeds of exchange transactions began to be accumulated by individuals and groups as a means of creating more wealth rather than as a means of display. The accumulated proceeds — that is, the financial sum of wealth — are called capital.

Capital is created and increased when resources are not consumed but saved for use in the creation of goods and services. Adam Smith argued that through the use of capital to mechanize industry, additional wealth and capital would be created, which would in turn be used for more economic growth and development that would benefit society. Karl Marx agreed with Smith that the marketplace for goods and services was the driving force in the creation of capital. The process by which additional wealth was created by the market became the focus of his economic study on the issue of accumulated wealth, *Das Kapital* (*Capital*). Marx (1867/1952) showed that capitalists use their capital to purchase raw materials, goods, and labor to transform these commodities into new goods and services.

Individuals and firms wishing to carry out productive activities must have access to capital to procure the goods, services, and labor necessary for that process. If individuals have previously accumulated capital on their own by consuming less wealth than they receive, the capital can be used for that purpose.

This is, of course, the situation found in the establishment of many small businesses. In this setting an individual uses money saved, his or her own capital, to buy goods or services to set up and operate his or her business. Because most individuals' capital is small, the resulting business's facilities, equipment, and size are small. The ability of such a firm to expand and grow is low because available capital is low. Many small newspapers, radio stations, magazines, and book publishers have been established by an individual's capital. If such a firm wishes to grow, additional capital must be obtained. The firm can save its pure profits for this purpose, but a lengthy time will be required to accumulate capital for expansion purposes.

In some cases, several individuals will create a larger pool of capital for such a business by joining into a partnership in which each shares the business and its proceeds. In such situations the amount of capital may still be low, and additional sources of capital may be sought to permit growth. Situations of this kind are often found in mid-sized publications, radio and television stations, and book firms.

The needs of capitalists for additional sources of capital for growth led to the development of two important mechanisms that accumulate capital and make it available to capitalists: capital lending and direct capital investing. Both mechanisms involve accumulating capital by individuals and making it available to other individuals or firms for productive uses in capital markets.

In capital lending, pools of capital are created by single individuals or groups of individuals and are loaned by capitalists for a fee. Traditional forms of this mechanism include loans from individuals and from thrift institutions such as banks, savings and loan associations, and credit unions. In direct capital investing, groups of individuals are brought together who contribute their capital to a firm in exchange for shares, that is, partial ownership of the firm. During the three-hundred-year development of capitalism, these lending and investment mechanisms have matured into large, well-established sources of capital represented by thrift institutions and stock exchanges. The availability of large amounts of capital through these sources has made it possible for huge firms with high productive capacities to develop in a way that an individual or small group of individuals could not have made possible through its own capital alone.

These two major sources of capital operate in separate capital markets and compete with each other in attracting financial resources to be used as capital and in making capital available to those who wish to use it for production and personal consumption. The amount of capital available in each market changes over time as those who save financial resources move them between the capital markets in order to gain the best return for the use of their money. General economic conditions, business trends, interest rates, and stock earnings affect decisions of where resources are placed by those with money available and decisions about price and other terms at which the accumulated capital is made available in the markets.

Capital obtained through loans is used by firms to create goods and services. When borrowing the capital, firms agree to repay the *principal*, that is, the amount borrowed, and to pay *interest*, that is, the cost for borrowing the capital. The borrower uses the capital to purchase raw materials, goods and services, and labor to produce a good or service and to sell that product to buyers. The revenue obtained is used to pay production costs, including the cost of the loan of capital, and, if the company is successful, to create pure profit and additional wealth that can be accumulated for the firm. The repayment of the principal and interest to the lending firm increases the wealth of the lender as well.

In a lending situation, lenders obviously are best served by receiving the highest possible interest on the capital that they lend and borrowers are best served when that rate for borrowing capital is as low as possible. If the price of capital rises too high, quantity demanded will diminish because many producers will not be able to pay the price and produce and sell their products at a price that will result in a profitable return. Likewise, if the price is too low, lenders will receive a small return and the opportunity costs for that use of the capital may lead them to use it in other ways.

The quantity of capital demanded and the supply of capital available at given prices are subject to the forces of supply and demand just like any good or service. The supply and demand for lent capital is thus based on price forces and also on other possible uses for capital, the state of the general economy, and government fiscal and monetary policies.

Nearly all media firms, large and small, borrow capital from thrift institutions as a means of stabilizing cash flow and purchasing new equipment and facilities. Larger firms regularly use such borrowed

Highlight 6.1 Public Media Companies
with Market Capitalization Exceeding $2 Billion

American Television and Communications
Capital Cities/ABC
Coca Cola
Columbia Broadcasting System
Disney
Dow Jones & Co.
Dun and Bradstreet
Gannett
Gulf and Western
Knight-Ridder
LIN
MCA
McGraw-Hill
News Corporation
New York Times Co.
Reuters
Tele-Communications Inc.
Time-Warner
Tribune
Times Mirror
Washington Post Co.

capital to finance expansion and to integrate their activities horizontally or vertically through the acquisition of other media firms.

When capital is directly invested in firms by individuals and other firms with accumulated capital, it is done with the desire to have the value of that capital increase through the profit and growth in the value of the firm in which it has been invested. Investment can be made in firms of all sizes, and the process is dictated by whether the firm is a *privately owned* or *publicly owned* corporation. Investments in private firms are made directly with the firm, and investments in public firms are made using brokerage houses that purchase shares in a stock market.

Privately owned firms tend to be smaller than publicly owned firms are because the former do not have high capital requirements or because they operate in limited product or geographic markets in local markets. In some cases they remain small because private firms' abilities to attract investment capital are lower than are those for public firms.

Investors purchase shares of firms that they believe will increase in value and will yield high dividends, that is, payments for profit earned.

The price at which investors are willing to purchase shares of a company is influenced by that company's financial position as well as market trends, technological developments, general economic developments, and other factors affecting perceptions of the state of the economy.

In such direct investment, investors purchase stock or shares in firms and select corporate directors and officers to manage the firms. Two major categories of stock are available: *common stock*, the largest category and primary type of stock, and *preferred stock*, which typically has no voting rights in the firm but has a guaranteed fixed rate of return or preference to assets over common stockholders if the company fails. Preferred stock is often purchased by persons who want a better return on capital than is available in thrift institutions but do not want the larger risk associated with common stock.

The value of a particular type of stock is indicated by three measures. The first measure is *par value*, which is the face value placed on the company shares when they are issued. The second indicator is *book value*, which is the accounting value of the stock to the firm, obtained by dividing a firm's net worth minus preferred stock by shares of common stock. Finally, there is *market value*, which is the actual price of one share if the share is purchased or sold. This value may be above or below book value depending upon investors' confidence, although it is normally close to or higher than book value.

In analyzing the value of firms based on their financial conditions, both direct investors and lenders pay particular attention to indicators of current growth and economic performance as well as past growth and economic performance of individual firms. Growth measures concentrate on growth of revenue, operating income, and assets over time, as well as consider what has happened in a firm in the past quarter or half year, or the past one, three, five, or ten years. Performance measures deal with profits, cash flows, and measures of the financial strength of firms, as well as *return on sales* (ROS), *return on assets* (ROA), and *return on investment* (ROI).

Indicators used in such financial analyses include measures of growth of revenue, cash flow, and assets. Performance measures include operating measures such as profit margins and sales-to-assets ratios, broader long-term analyses such as ratios of assets to liabilities, liquid assets to current liabilities, capitalization, and indicators of the return on investment such as return on equity and price-earnings ratios. Media companies have done very well in terms of growth and performance in recent years, typically exceeding or even doubling the growth and return rates of nonmedia firms (Table 6.1).

The general financial efficiency of a firm is displayed by its *operating profit margin*, which indicates the firm's profit as a percent of sales

TABLE 6.1 Average Growth Rates in the Mid-1980s

Industry	Revenues	Assets
Book publishing	9	16
Broadcasting (TV & radio)	13	24
Cable & pay TV	31	27
Entertainment programming	18	17
Magazines — consumer	8	24
Magazines — business	7	10
Newspaper publishing	11	14
Audio recordings	3	7

Average Performance Measures

Industry	Op. Income Margin %	Return on Total Assets %
Book publishing	10	14
Broadcasting (TV & radio)	18	18
Cable & pay TV	17	9
Entertainment programming	11	9
Magazines — consumer	10	23
Magazines — business	12	26
Newspaper publishing	17	26
Audio recordings	7	14

before accounting for interest payments and taxes. *Current ratio* reports the current assets to current liabilities, a measure that provides a view of the current financial strength of the firm. Generally a firm likes to have a two-to-one ratio. *Liquidity ratio* indicates the amount of cash, securities, and other liquid assets on hand, that is, assets that can be turned into cash without significant loss of value, in comparison to the current liabilities of the company. When firms acquire other firms or make capital expenditures for new facilities or equipment, the liquidity ratio can be expected to be lower than normal.

Capitalization ratios indicate the percentage of capital represented by preferred and common stock and long-term debt. *Sales to assets* ratios provide an indicator of how well company revenues are being used. *Inventory turnover* indicates how many times the inventory of a firm has turned over during a year. This measure is most often used in dealing with retail businesses, but also has bearing on the activities of book and audio and visual recording firms.

Financial analyses also consider the *return on investment* provided by firms. Such measures consider the pure profits, sometimes before and sometimes after reinvestment, that accrue to company owners. *Return on equity* is an important indicator that reports the net income

Highlight 6.2 Calculation of Growth and Performance Measures

Growth Measures

Annual Growth of Revenue (expressed as percentage)

$$\frac{\text{Latest Year's Revenue} - \text{Previous Year's Revenue}}{\text{Previous Year's Revenue}}$$

Annual Growth of Operating Income (expressed as percentage)

$$\frac{\text{Latest Year's Operating Income} - \text{Previous Year's Operating Income}}{\text{Previous Year's Operating Income}}$$

Annual Growth of Assets (expressed as percentage)

$$\frac{\text{Latest Year's Assets} - \text{Previous Year's Assets}}{\text{Previous Year's Assets}}$$

Annual Growth of Net Worth (expressed as percentage)

$$\frac{\text{Latest Year's Net Worth} - \text{Previous Year's Net Worth}}{\text{Previous Year's Net Worth}}$$

Liquidity Measures

Current Ratio

$$\frac{\text{Current Assets}}{\text{Current Liabilities}}$$

Acid Test Ratio

$$\frac{\text{Liquid Assets}}{\text{Current Liabilities}}$$

Profitability Measures

Return on Sales

$$\frac{\text{Operating Income}}{\text{Revenue}}$$

Return on Assets

$$\frac{\text{Operating Income}}{\text{Total Assets}} \quad \text{or} \quad \frac{\text{Operating Income}}{\text{Fixed Assets}}$$

Return on Equity (expressed as percentage)

$$\frac{\text{Operating Income}}{\text{Net Worth}}$$

Price-Earnings Ratio

$$\frac{\text{Market Price of a Share}}{\text{Earnings of the Share}}$$

Highlight 6.2 (continued)

Financial Strength Measures

Operating Profit Margin (expressed as percentage)

$$\frac{\text{Operating Income (Before Taxes and Interest Payments)}}{\text{Operating Revenue}}$$

Cash Flow Margin (expressed as percentage)

$$\frac{\text{Operating Income (Before Taxes and Interest Payments)} + \text{depreciation and amortization}}{\text{Operating Revenue}}$$

Capitalization Ratio (expressed as percentage)

$$\frac{\text{Preferred Stock}}{\text{Common Stock}} \text{ or } \frac{\text{Long–Term Debt}}{\text{Common Stock}}$$

Debt to Equity

$$\frac{\text{Total Debt}}{\text{Total Equity}}$$

---

of a firm as a percentage of the net worth of a firm. This yields a measure of how much the company is earning compared to the value of the investors' shares. The *price-earnings ratio* indicates the relationship of the price of the firm's shares in the stock market to the earnings per share.

ISSUES OF MEDIA PERFORMANCE AND CAPITAL MARKETS

Although media owners have always been concerned with financial performance and the availability of capital from thrift institutions, it has only been in recent decades that they have entered the market for direct investment capital as publicly owned corporations. This new form of capitalization has resulted in significant changes in the management and size of firms.

Prior to the development of television and cable systems, the number of public companies was low. Even after the development of television broadcasting, public companies tended to be limited to networks and television programs and motion picture companies. The development of cable television with its high capital costs for equipment and installation resulted in the formation of large firms with public corporate ownership to accumulate the capital necessary to build and operate such firms. In the 1970s, newspaper firms that had typically operated under proprietorships and private corporation structures began to turn to public corporate ownership as a means of expansion. The Gannett Co. became the leading newspaper firm and a model of how privately owned newspaper companies could go public and use the additional capital for rapid expansion.

The literature about these developments and analysis of their effects has been limited for the most part to anecdotal and popular studies of media developments. Contributions in this regard include studies by Michael Leapman (1984) and Thomas Kiernan (1986) of Rupert Murdoch's News Corporation, and Edward Scharff's study of the *Wall Street Journal* (1988). Broadcast studies have included one on the role of William Paley in the development of CBS (Paper, 1987), and another on how the financial takeover of CBS affected that firm's news operations (McCabe, 1987). There have also been reviews by McClintick (1982), Litwak (1986), and Yule (1988) of the influence of firms, markets, and individuals on motion picture industry financing. Another of this type of study explored Time Incorporated's disastrous attempt to start a broadcast and cable television magazine (Byron, 1986). Broader studies of the impact of major public companies on media industries have been made by Bagdikian (1987) and Schiller (1981).

It has only been in recent years that a more specialized scholarly and applied literature on the financial performance of, and capital markets for, media companies has developed. Methods for analyzing media company performance and value have been the focus of Wolpert and Wolpert (1986), and studies of financial performance of communications firms such as *Communications Industry Report, Broadcast Stats, Duncan's Radio Market Guide, Radio Financial Report, Investing in Radio, Investing in Television,* and *Kagan Cable TV Financial Databook* are available.

Use of financial growth and performance data for management and investment decisions became a significant topic of media management books in the last part of the 1980s, reflecting the new importance attached by the industry and capital markets to financial performance. Exploration of the importance of profit-and-loss statements, balance sheets, and market information, as well as discussions of how to use such data, has been made in texts by Marcus (1986); Fink (1988); O'Donnell, Hausman, and Benoit (1989); and Lavine and Wackman (1988). Some industry associations and investment firms have produced materials on how to use such data in making investment and management decisions as well, including the National Association of

Broadcasters (1978) and the Institute of Newspaper Controllers and Finance Officers (1975).

A study by McGann and Russell (1988) of publicly owned broadcast firms found that, despite fears fueled by the CBS takeover and the sale of ABC to Capital Cities Communications in the mid-1980s, broadcast firms were well defended against unwanted takeovers, and that their financial performance was better than that for companies in nonmedia industries.

7

GOVERNMENT INTERVENTION IN THE MARKET

Government regularly intervenes in media markets to promote social goals and influence the market conduct of media firms. This chapter reviews the concepts of efficiency, equity, and externalities and how they affect government decisions to intervene. Intervention occurs through regulation, advantages, and subsidies.

Governments intervene in markets to put into place public policies that override or supplement the allocative decisions of market mechanisms, promote competition, and protect emerging industries. These policies are intended to protect producers and consumers or to meet social needs, or to be political responses to pressures brought to bear by producers and consumers. Media companies regularly encounter government intervention. When WIVB-TV applied for a renewal of its license to broadcast in Buffalo, it was because the government had intervened in the structure of the broadcast market. When the Environmental Protection Agency issued regulations requiring newspapers to analyze their ink waste for hazardous chemicals and to dispose of such chemicals properly, the government was intervening in the market. When the Detroit *Free Press* and *News* applied to the Justice Department to form a joint operating agreement, they did so because the government had intervened in the market with antitrust laws that normally prohibit such joint operations.

At the macroeconomic level, capitalist governments intervene to provide currency and raise taxes for economic and social infrastructures, to respond to economic and social ills (such as inflation, unemployment, and poverty) and to stimulate or retard their economies. At the microeconomic level, governments intervene to promote industries and commerce and to respond to market problems in industries by instituting policies that promote desirable outcomes and inhibit undesirable outcomes.

All capitalist nations, despite their market-based economies, intervene and engage in economic planning activities, but not to the extent of centrally planned economies. There are no market capitalist nations that adhere to laissez-faire policies with regard to the economic market. Capitalist nations intervene by engaging in *simple monopoly capitalism* or *state monopoly capitalism.* Simple monopoly capitalism is a condition in which the state engages in low levels of central planning and directs most of its intervention as a means of promoting economic activity. State monopoly capitalism exists when governments override the operation of the market through taxes, public ownership, and monetary policies that provide them extensive control over the market.

Capitalist government decisions to intervene or leave markets alone are made on the basis of *welfare economics.* Welfare economics focuses on the behavior of firms or industries and how it affects their performance. Welfare economics is concerned with the issues of *efficiency, equity,* and *externalities.*

Efficiency is concerned with whether the actions of firms maximize total wealth, measured in terms of *allocative efficiency* and *technical efficiency.* Allocative efficiency deals with the market decisions involving allocation and seeks to ensure that excess profits are not earned by producers and that the pressures of consumers and producers on the market function so that the market can operate at optimal points that spread its benefits between producers, between consumers, and between producers and consumers. Technical efficiency deals with whether the inputs used are used most effectively to maximize output.

Equity is concerned with the manner in which the total wealth is distributed among producers and consumers. In a market-based system, the wealth needs to be distributed among all producers and consumers in a fashion that promotes the interests of both groups and the interests of the society as a whole. If distribution is too equal — as in centrally planned economies or market economies with unduly high taxes used to redistribute wealth — a loss of incentive for producers to produce wealth beyond what one would receive can be expected since that surplus would be taken away and given to others.

Externalities involve results of activities in the market that affect society outside the market itself. These include environmental and social effects of production and consumption.

In making decisions to intervene, governments are influenced by the interaction of efficiency and equity and the externalities that are present. If significant inefficiencies exist, government may intervene. This often occurs when monopolies and oligopolies are present and create allocative inefficiency that also harms equity. Under such conditions producers can restrict output and thus increase price or fix price higher than output would normally produce. Thus the producers receive excessive profits. This, of course, redistributes the wealth from consumers to producers in a way that does not maximize economic well-being. Technical inefficiencies that occur when output is not maximized result in higher cost to consumers and redistribution of wealth toward producers that is harmful, so governments sometimes intervene by making bulk purchases of goods beyond what the market demands in order to improve technical efficiency.

If externalities exist, governments may intervene to stop harmful externalities, to ameliorate the damage caused by harmful externalities, or to protect and promote beneficial externalities.

The issues of efficiency and equity, and government intervention to promote the two, are especially important in terms of media because of the important social roles that media play in a democratic society. Although it may be desirable for government to promote these purposes, it becomes undesirable when the intervention inhibits media activities that carry out those social roles. As a result, there is a tension created whenever government intervenes, as well as concern over its potential impact on society.

When governments decide to intervene in economic markets, they do so with four major types of intervention: 1) regulation; 2) advantages; 3) subsidies; and 4) taxation.

Regulation of industry occurs in three ways. First, there is technical regulation, such as the setting and maintenance of industry standards and control of commonly used thoroughfares in order to ensure compatibility, quality, and safety. Second, governments intervene with market structure regulation. They do so in order to control the number of producers and sellers and to attempt to diversify market structure. Among the methods used for structure regulation are franchises and licenses in which certain types of structures are permitted or protected. Third, governments use behavioral regulation that controls the acts of firms, such as preventing anticompetitive action that might harm the market, controlling rates and prices in efforts to achieve macroeconomic goals, or controlling harmful externalities.

When in place, regulations have economic effects. These involve increases or decreases in costs, revenues, or profits caused by the addition of nonmarket requirements and forces.

Advantages are preferred treatment by government or the provision of reduced prices for government services, those provided by government-regulated industries, or agencies related to government. Advantages may be given to all industries or may target specific industries that governments wish to aid. Included in this category of intervention are tax breaks and exemptions from regulation. The economic effect of advantages reduces the costs of production, thus increasing profit for a firm or raising it to the point where the additional profit is an incentive for production.

Subsidies are cash transfers from government to industries to promote an industry or type of production. They can also be provided as an incentive to halt harmful externalities or to pay for equipment that will halt them. Subsidies increase revenue, thus increasing profit or creating incentives for production.

Taxation involves cash transfers from producers or consumers to government to pay for government activities, but it is also used as a means of penalizing firms for undesirable externalities and providing government money to ameliorate such problems.

Subsidies and advantages can be classed as direct or indirect aid. They are *direct* when they involve specific assistance to an individual media unit, such as a firm subsidy or grant given to a production company. Intervention is considered *indirect* if it is provided across a class of media or other business units, such as tax advantages that are enjoyed by broadcasting and newspaper groups and other media firms for acquisition of new properties.

Intervention may also be *specific*; that is, it may be undertaken by government to promote a clearly stated goal or to help achieve a specified output, as in the case of research grants provided to support newspaper industry efforts to replace wood pulp in newsprint with kenas. Other intervention is considered *general*, that is, aid to promote generally the health or development of a media industry or industry as a whole, such as tax advantages that exempt advertising sales from sales or professional taxes in most states.

Finally, intervention may be mandated or selective. *Mandated intervention* is authorized by law, and government administrators do not have a choice in granting or withholding the intervention, such as in the case of regulating electromagnetic spectrum or providing a tax credit on a tax return. *Selective intervention* involves intervention that is made at the discretion of an official or officials, such as decisions of state or federal antitrust agencies to prosecute anticompetitive actions by firms, or loans can be provided to media by agencies such as the Small Business Administration.

INTERVENTION IN MEDIA ECONOMICS

Government intervention in media economics occurs through all the mechanisms discussed above: regulation, advantages, subsidies, and taxation.

The three types of regulation — technical, market structure, and behavioral — are justified as means of protecting the public welfare and ensuring that the market can operate effectively. Technical regulation occurs in the setting of broadcast and cablecast technical standards—mechanical standards for equipment used in printing and production of video and audio products. It occurred when Congress required television sets to be built with both UHF and VHF channels on them. It also occurs in the assignment and protection of electromagnetic frequencies.

Market structure regulation occurs in the granting of broadcast licenses and cable franchises; in antitrust actions aimed at controlling vertical and horizontal integration and the development of monopoly in specific markets; and in the provision of loans, grants, and other funding to promote media and diverse ownership that would not exist or survive if left to market forces alone. Structural regulation is seen in rules prohibiting cross-ownership of certain media and limiting multiple ownership of broadcasting stations, and in antitrust laws prohibiting motion picture producers from owning exhibition houses.

Behavioral regulation occurs through the determination of acceptable practices for broadcasting and cablecasting, including efforts to halt externalities that result in regulation of offensive speech in television and radio broadcasts, and regulation of sexual content of films, videos, books, and magazines. Regulations are used to control the externalities of pollutants resulting from chemicals, ink, and petroleum products used in printing newspapers and magazines. Regulations are also evidenced by antitrust laws regulating conduct such as price fixing, predatory pricing, and market allocation that harms the ability of media markets to operate effectively.

Much writing and research on the regulation of media has focused upon its real and imagined conflicts with libertarian ideals. Only a few studies have significantly explored its economic bases.

Government intervention through antitrust enforcement and judicial decisions in antitrust litigation present significant issues. Busterna (1988a) has shown that in the 1980s little federal enforcement of antitrust statutes involving newspapers has occurred; rather, antitrust activity has tended to be litigation between newspapers over each other's practices, mainly in the area of advertising pricing and practices. Antitrust enforcement has traditionally been much more vigorously exercised in the motion picture industry than in other media industries and has resulted in an early splitting of production and exhibition activities (Conant, 1978).

Recent acquisitions have begun again to integrate vertically the motion picture industry through acquisition of cable and theater firms by conglomerate owners of production companies. Concurrently, there has been increasing concentration in the motion picture exhibition portion of the industry, but these developments have not yet resulted in strong antitrust intervention by the government (Guback, 1987).

The use of antitrust laws to keep program producers out of joint ventures with cable operators and the need for concern about vertical integration of the cable television industry have been asserted by White (1985), but antitrust enforcement has been minimal in the 1980s, according to Chan-Olmsted and Litman (1988). Their research indicates that horizontal acquisitions in the cable industry have been generally ignored by the Justice Department and that as the result of horizontal and vertical mergers, cable programming companies have gained significant ownership of local cable systems representing the exhibition stage of the industry. As they have done so, the companies have begun exercising significant market power.

The effects of government regulatory policies on broadcasting economics have been of significant interest, especially in terms of the control of local and national audiences that regulation has provided to certain broadcasters and networks. Levin (1971) argued that government licensing and control of the electromagnetic spectrum unduly limited the development of broadcasting and other spectrum-based communication services and provided abnormal financial returns to broadcasters between the 1930s and 1950s. He argued that the market constraints should be limited, thus opening up competition that benefits consumers; that the government should provide incentives to develop use of the spectrum; and that the subsidy of free spectrum use should be eliminated. Owen (1975) argued that broadcasting companies had managed to direct government regulation of broadcasting to promote and protect their profit. In both broadcasting and cable, government regulation was used to limit competition and available spectrum space, and no incentives were provided to improve performance or to promote operating in the public interest. Owen's argument was underscored by Noll et al. (1973), who argued that government policies toward broadcasting needed alteration because they have provided undue economic advantages to broadcasters that have harmed the public welfare, particularly by shielding them from competition and making them unduly profitable.

A later study by Owen (1978) considered the dominance of television networks in terms of programming and suggested that regulatory policies promoting alternative programming sources and reducing network control over the television market could be achieved by altering the industry structure set up by existing government regulation. Levin (1980) concurred in his exploration of the history of government regulation of television and its effects. He supported changes in policies to encourage the availability of multiple channels in broadcast markets, to improve the quality of programming, and to promote diversity.

Disputes over policies that regulate other market structures, such as the FCC's prohibition of ownership of a newspaper and broadcast property in the same geographic market, have also resulted in significant discussion but little research. Owen (1975) has noted that cross-ownership prohibitions are a form of antitrust enforcement in regulated industries.

Advantages involve a variety of public policy decisions that help promote media industries. Included are tax advantages, such as the exemption of advertising from sales taxes on services in most states, and postal rate advantages under which newspapers, magazines, books, and advertising material can be mailed at special reduced rates. Also included in this category are provisions such as the Newspaper Preservation Act, that has exempted some newspapers from antitrust laws. Advantages are often requested and extended because they promote the beneficial externalities of free flow of information and an informed public, and the attendant social benefits that are presumed to arise from these externalities.

The major advantage, made early in the United States, was to reduce the cost of sending newspapers and other printed material through the mail. This fiscal advantage was a means of promoting the health of publishers and public welfare by keeping the cost of acquiring information low, but, according to Kielbowicz (1986), was also made as a means of currying publishers' favor in the late nineteenth century.

Government intervention caused by the exemption of joint operating newspapers from antitrust laws by the Newspaper Preservation Act has been a significant area of concern. Worries about its potential impact were raised by Barnett (1969) and Malone (1969) prior to its passage. Since that time, its actual economic impact has been studied by a number of observers. In order to determine failure in a paper, five major economic and financial tests have been applied under the Act, according to Picard (1987). These arrangements have also created significant concern that public welfare is being sacrificed for the sake of a few newspaper producers. That concern has been well-articulated by Barnett (1980) and Carlson (1982) — who argued that the Act created extensive barriers to entry and allowed harmful anticompetitive acts — and by Barwis (1980), who asserted that the preservation of separate voices was not dependent upon granting such a monopoly and that it unduly shields newspapers from economic forces. More recently, Busterna (1988c) argued that the broad antitrust exemption provided by the Act is harmful to consumers, a view agreed upon by Picard (1988c), who has argued for revision of the act to remove the most flagrant anticompetitive actions in order to protect the public, while at the same

Highlight 7.1 Four Propositions about State Intervention in Press Economics

---

1. The character of state intervention in press economics depends upon the nature of the relationship between the state and its citizens. When citizens are subservient to the state . . . intervention will be authoritarian and seductive and will be used to gain the press's acquiescence. As states become more democratic and individual liberty increases, the intervention becomes less coercive.

2. State intervention expands and contracts in accordance to the economic needs of the press. The amount of intervention is determined by the press's financial stability. Intervention will increase to meet the press's minimum financial requirements and will decrease when these requirements are satisfied by outside sources.

3. The types of state intervention are shaped by the political-economic tenets accepted in a particular nation. The dominant political and economic philosophies, or their accepted interpretations, will determine the nature and forms of intervention in a given state, regardless of the forms of intervention selected by other states at comparable levels of economic and democratic development.

4. In any given nation, state intervention in press economics will parallel intervention in the economy as a whole. State press policies will be consistent with economic policies pursued in other industries and in the general economy.

(Picard, 1985b, pp. 124-125)

---

time allowing the economies of scale from joint operations to continue as a means of cost sharing between joint operating papers.

Subsidies to media in the United States are not as great as in other nations but include research grants to improve journalistic and production techniques and to fund research on improvements in the use of basic resources. Subsidies also include purchases of media products by government, such as broadcast programming for armed services and bulk purchases of newspapers and magazines for government employees.

Smith (1977) and Hollstein (1978) explored increasing government subsidies to newspapers in European nations during the 1970s, arguing that the policies were based on the need to improve access to media, reduce newspaper mortality, and halt concentration of ownership. Picard (1985a) found four main patterns of intervention in newspaper economics among Western nations and asserted that the patterns were related to the general macroeconomic policies of the nations, suggesting propositions that link press policies to the macroeconomic policies and political relationships of the society (Picard, 1985b).

Mayer (1973) revealed how many nations, especially Western European countries and Canada, have provided subsidies to motion picture producers as a means of promoting their national film industries. In many cases, these subsidies are funded with taxes on theater admissions.

Taxation has not been a significant form of intervention in U.S. media because taxes that are not general taxes levied on all businesses have usually been found to be unconstitutional if applied only to media. Much discussion, however, has focused on the application of tax advantages as a means of promoting desirable industry structures. In recent years, concern over video and audiotape has led to efforts to tax these products as a means of providing compensation pools for producers of video and audio recordings who are not compensated when consumers record available copies for their own use. Breenan (1988) has argued against taxation of home audiotapes as a means of compensating record companies and recording artists whose work is copied by individuals for personal use, maintaining that a tax would not provide sufficient benefits to warrant the intervention.

In a study of tax policies affecting newspapers, Dertouzous and Thorpe (1982) found that inheritance and capital gains taxes, combined with tax advantages for the acquisitions of newspapers, are the primary causes of the decline of independent newspaper ownership. Their research revealed that existing tax policies provide economic incentives to both independent newspaper owners and newspaper groups — incentives that promote acquisition of papers by groups. For the trend away from independent ownership to be slowed, changes in tax laws would be required.

8

LABOR IN THE MARKET

Media could not exist without the contributions of employees and managers. This chapter discusses how media become consumers when they employ labor, the influences on labor supply and demand, and the contributions that labor makes to production. It reviews how labor supply is affected by compensation offered, work type, and labor organization.

Labor is an important factor in production. Media industries that rely heavily on human resources must pay a significant amount of attention to their role. Economic issues, including the amount of labor available, wages paid, the quality of labor, and how additional labor increases output, are particularly important in understanding the economics and management of media firms.

Media are labor intensive. Labor is one of the most expensive inputs in media production. The resource is available from an independent labor market made up of individuals selling their labor and companies willing to purchase the labor. Media companies seek labor from a general market for basic, unskilled labor, as well as from markets for labor with specialized technical and creative abilities. When the Minneapolis *Star & Tribune* hires a printer, or Universal Studios hires a carpenter, or ABC News hires a news producer, each enters one of these labor markets as a consumer.

Like other markets, the labor market is influenced by basic economic laws such as the law of supply and demand. The supply of labor available for a given job and overall is influenced by the wages or salaries that employers are willing to pay, and the demand for that labor is influenced by the price at which the labor is made available.

LABOR SUPPLY

The quantity of labor available in the market is also affected by two major nonprice factors: the number of workers in the labor force and the amount of time each laborer works. The number of workers in the labor force varies over time depending upon the size of the population,

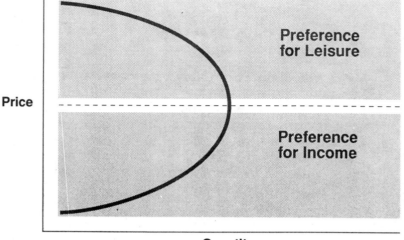

Figure 8.1 Supply Curve for Labor

the average age of the citizens, and social changes that influence the number of individuals willing and able to work. When a nation's population increases or decreases, one can expect the pool of workers to vary proportionately. Changes in the average age of a population also affect the number of workers. If the average age of the population changes, more or fewer of the population will be of working age and this will affect the size of the labor force. When society forbade child labor, the work force size was reduced, just as acceptance of women into the general labor market increased the pool of laborers. The number of hours of work in which workers will engage also affects labor supply. A reduction in the length of the average workday and workweek thus decreases the number of hours of labor available.

In broad terms all workers choose whether to enter the labor market and the amount of time they will contribute in the market. The supply curve for labor is different from the supply curve of other goods and services, but the supply of labor is strongly affected by price (see Figure 8.1).

The backward-bending supply curve occurs because workers are not willing to increase continually the number of hours of work they contribute to the labor market. Although increasing the number of hours of labor increases the total income workers receive, the additional income is more desirable than leisure time only up to the point that the marginal utility of income begins diminishing.

Labor itself involves inherent disutility for most individuals and is undertaken merely as a means of gaining income that can be used for consumption of goods and services that provide utility. As a result, when labor is increased the disutility increases and marginal disutility increases rapidly. Because of this, the number of hours of labor made available in the market will increase as price increases only to the point that the desire for income outweighs the desire for leisure. At that point the number of hours of labor available at even higher prices stabilizes and then diminishes into the backward-bending curve. Thus, a newspaper editor cannot expect that his reporters will be willing to work long overtime hours continually even if they receive additional pay and the general manager of a radio station cannot expect an engineer to do the same thing on a regular basis.

In addition to quantitative factors, the productivity of labor obtained from the market is influenced by qualitative factors. These include human capital, shifts in occupational choices, and worker motivation. Human capital includes the skills and knowledge of workers in the labor force. When workers are highly trained and schooled, their ability to produce productively — that is, their human capital — is increased. Thus, their productive *capacity* is higher and the amount of labor needed to produce the same output is lower than it is for less skilled workers. Firms recognize the impact of trained personnel on productivity and thus seek such skilled labor when hiring, and many conduct internal training to raise the skills and abilities and, consequently, productivity of labor.

Increases in the quality and quantity of labor available elevate the potential productivity of firms, as seen in Figure 8.2. This potential productivity assumes that the labor will continue to be used efficiently and that the marginal physical product will increase proportionately. Because of the law of diminishing returns, however, the productivity will at some point reach a plateau and even decline.

The labor market is also affected by the nonmonetary income, that is, psychic income, that workers receive or do not receive from specific labor. Some occupations provide psychological rewards or satisfactions — such as prestige, power, camaraderie, or a feeling of serving society — that may influence the supply of labor for those occupations by increasing the amount of labor available despite the price paid for the labor. Such is the case in the labor market for actors and journalists, where a high supply of workers exists despite the low price paid for labor.

The amount and quality of labor available are also influenced by the geographic location of available employment and workers and the

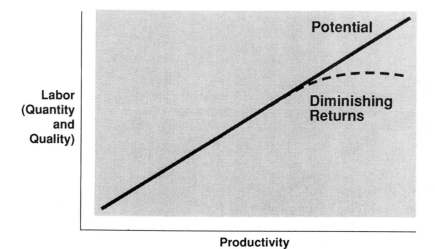

Figure 8.2 The Influence of Increase in Labor Quantity and Quality on Production

degree of mobility to other occupations. For example, a television station in Bozeman, Montana, is a less desirable location for reporters than is a television station in Washington, DC. As a result, the amount and quality of reporting labor in the labor pool for the Bozeman station will be lower than that for the Washington station.

DEMAND FOR LABOR

Demand for labor is, as mentioned above, affected by the price of labor, but it is also affected by decreasing demand for the product produced caused by changes in the price of the product or changes in consumer preferences or tastes. This is illustrated, for example, by the decreasing demand for labor in network television as audiences for broadcast television have shifted to cable television.

Changes in the inputs of production that alter productivity can also affect demand for labor. The introduction of technology that increases the productivity of labor reduces the need for labor. This has been clearly shown by Dertouzous and Quinn (1985), who studied the impact of electronic technology on newspaper labor requirements and found that it reduced the amount of production labor required by at least half. They concluded, however, that few employees were laid off as a result of the transition, but that most of the excess labor was reduced through attrition, buyouts, and retraining.

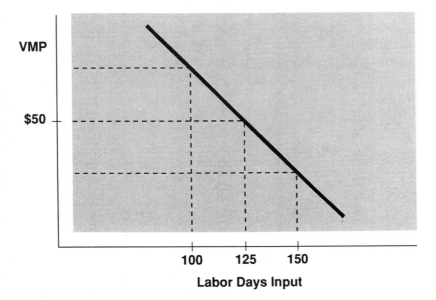

Figure 8.3 Labor Demand Curve Calculated by Value of Marginal Product

When a product and labor market is operating most efficiently under perfect competition, the supply and demand for labor equalize as indicated above. In order to calculate demand for labor in such a situation, one establishes the value of the marginal product (VMP), that is, the value of the additional output achieved by adding a unit of labor. This value is calculated as follows:

$$\text{Value of marginal product} = \text{Price} \times \text{Marginal physical product of labor}$$

A firm will continue adding labor to the point that the value of the marginal product no longer exceeds the price of the input. If a newspaper had an MPP of 200 newspapers that could be delivered by carriers daily and the price of the papers was 25 cents each, the VMP would be $50 a day. Assume that the paper pays carriers the $50 to deliver the papers. Figure 8.3 illustrates that the VMP of the 100th carrier hired would be well above $50 and the firm would get more income than the cost of delivering the papers. This firm would thus wish to hire at least 100 carriers and possibly more. A firm will normally add units of labor until the VMP decreases to the price of the input. If more carriers were hired, the VMP would decline because of the law of diminishing returns. Because the VMP of $50 for the 125th

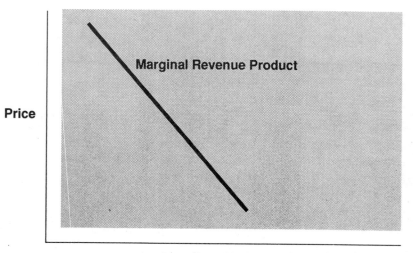

Quantity of Labor Input

Figure 8.4 Labor Demand Curve for Firms in Imperfect Competition
(Indicated by Marginal Revenue Product)

carrier still meets labor cost, the firm would be expected to hire 125 carriers. If it stopped before that point, it would lose the additional profits indicated by the shaded area. If more than 125 carriers were employed, however, the VMP would decline below cost and the firm would lose money by adding labor.

In situations where product competition is imperfect, the product demand curve slopes downward and the marginal revenue received from each additional product unit is less than the cost of the unit itself because producers must lower their price in order to sell additional units produced, with the cost of the losses on marginal product spread across all units produced. In such imperfectly competitive situations, the demand curve for labor is analyzed by calculating the value of the additional product, using marginal revenue product (MRP):

$$\text{MRP} = \text{Marginal revenue} \times \frac{\text{Marginal physical}}{\text{product of labor}}$$

Marginal revenue product declines rapidly because of diminishing returns, and the marginal revenue is lower than cost (see Figure 8.4). As a result, the demand curve for labor in firms in imperfect competition declines more rapidly than that for firms in perfect competition and the benefits of additional labor disappear more rapidly.

THE PRICE OF LABOR

In a perfectly competitive market for labor, the price paid for labor will be determined by the law of supply and demand, and the price is determined just as the price is for any product in such a market.

Some firms will be willing to pay more for less than the equilibrium price set by the forces of supply and demand. This occurs because some firms wish to acquire the most experienced and skilled workers, while others are willing to provide entry-level jobs at low pay in which workers gain or improve their skills. This is clearly the case in the broadcast and newspaper industries where young or new workers begin work in small stations and papers that pay very low wages; on the other end of the spectrum are stations such as KABC-TV in Los Angeles and newspapers such as the New York *Times*, which pay far above the price for the nationwide media labor market.

At times the labor market can be imperfect and tilt in favor of sellers or buyers. This occurs when the market contains a limited number of workers with necessary skills or when buyers have advantages because of high unemployment or because few other employers exist in the market.

Trade unions and professional societies bring important forces to bear on the economic marketplace by altering supply and demand for labor. The major goals of such groups are to improve working conditions and increase wages or salaries of employees. To do so, industrial and craft unions and professional societies attempt to influence labor supply and demand to increase the price paid for the members' labor.

Such efforts are undertaken by two major strategies. First, unions and similar societies strive to increase the price paid for labor by reducing labor supply. This is usually done by limiting entry into the labor market by requiring apprenticeships, specialized training, and licenses, and by limiting entry into such programs. Newspaper press unions and electrical workers in motion picture and broadcasting industries often limit labor through these tactics. Second, some labor groups work to increase demand for labor by increasing job specializations, by overmanning, and by increasing labor productivity by improving the quality of labor. This strategy is employed by printers' unions and certain broadcasting unions.

Related to these strategies is collective bargaining, in which unions work to achieve wages that are higher than would normally be achieved by supply and demand alone. Under collective bargaining, workers attempt to limit labor in an industry to members of unions, thus requiring all producers to employ higher-priced labor and thus equally increasing the cost of labor inputs so that no firm gains an advantage by using lower-priced labor. Collective bargaining has been effectively used by groups such as the Screen Actors' Guild, the Writers' Guild, the American Federation of Television and Radio Artists, and the Newspaper Guild.

Unions, too, pay close attention to economics in their collective bargaining effects, cognizant that if the price of labor is artificially raised too high, producers will be forced either to reduce labor hired because the price paid to workers for marginal output will exceed the value of the output or to move production to other nations where labor can be obtained cheaper or without collective bargaining. As a result, the ability of labor groups to bargain is somewhat constrained because members of these groups do not wish to risk significant layoffs as a result of demanding increasing raises.

The strategies employed in collective bargaining in media and the impact and development of broadcasting unions in the U.S. have been explored by Koenig (1970), and studies of British unions by Beharrell and Philo (1977) and by Seglow (1978) provide comparative views. This literature, while dealing with economic issues, concentrates on bargaining and managerial issues.

Few important economic studies of the role of labor in media industries have been made, and the scholarly literature is nearly devoid of such contributions. Literature relating to managerial issues of labor is abundant but, for the most part, ignores economic analysis and is concerned primarily with issues such as different educational and training methods, comparative salary surveys, and management of personnel.

SOME FINAL WORDS

This book has provided an introduction to the concepts that are basic to an understanding of media economics and a review of some of the issues and research in the field. It is by no means complete because researchers and practitioners have only recently begun to study the field significantly and recognize the need for understanding of the principles and issues.

It is hoped that this book will help stimulate that understanding as well as more research and analysis of issues in the field. Such interest can only lead to improved decision making in the operations of media, a greater understanding of the economic forces that affect media institutions, and an improved base of knowledge to apply in the making of public policy decisions about media.

This book is intended to provide a starting point for such interest and analysis. There is much to be done in terms of the economic study of media. As the reviews of recent research in each chapter have revealed, there are large gaps in the literature and great opportunities for both applied and theoretical research in the field.

The literature reviewed here has focused on the recent developments in the field and the current state of knowledge. Scholarship about media economics is clearly incomplete and significant work needs to be undertaken to add to the literature of consumer demand for media, media supply, cost issues, market structure effects, and financial and labor issues.

If the readers of this book, however, merely use the information conveyed to understand what differences exist in media markets, how media compete, how audiences and advertisers select media and the economic factors that influence their selections, what the cost and revenue factors are that need to be considered when media managers make production decisions, how government activities influence media economics, how to analyze the economic performance of media, and what factors influence the availability and price of labor, they will have a much stronger comprehension of the forces that shape media industries and a greater ability to make knowledgeable choices should they be placed in decision-making positions in media.

Those who wish to find contemporary data and information about media economics to improve their understanding as media professionals, critics, or scholars should find the various trade, labor, and media service firms and publications in the resources listing at the rear of this book useful. Also of interest should be the listing of early contributions in the field of media economics, the references, and the glossary.

RESOURCES FOR MEDIA ECONOMICS DATA

TRADE AND LABOR GROUPS AND MEDIA SERVICE FIRMS

American Advertising Federation, 1400 K Street, N.W., Suite 100, Washington, DC 20005 Tele.: (201) 898-0089

American Association of Advertising Agencies, 666 Third Avenue, 13th Floor, New York, NY 10017 Tele.: (212) 682-2500

American Business Press, 205 E. 42nd Street, New York, NY 10017 Tele.: (212) 661-6360

American Federation of Television and Radio Artists, 1350 Avenue of the Americas, New York, NY 10019 Tele.: (212)265-7700

American Newspaper Publishers Association, P.O. Box 17407, Dulles Airport, Washington, DC 20041 Tele.: (703) 648-1247

American Video Association, 557 E. Juanita, #3, Mesa, AZ 85204 Tele.: (602) 892-8553

Arbitron Co., 1350 Avenue of the Americas, New York, NY 10019 Tele.: (212) 887-1300

Association of Alternative Newsweeklies, 2 NW Second Avenue, Portland, OR 97209 Tele.: (503) 243-2122

Association of Business Publishers, 205 E. 42nd Street, New York, NY 10017 Tele.: (212) 661-6360

Association of Independent Television Stations, 1200 18th Street, N.W., Suite 502, Washington, DC 20036 Tele.: (202) 887-1970

Association of National Advertisers, 155 E. 44th Street, New York, NY 10007 Tele.: (212)697-5950

Audit Bureau of Circulations, 900 N. Meacham Road, Schaumburg, IL 60195 Tele.: (312)885-0910

Birch Radio, Inc., 44 Sylvan Avenue, #2D, Englewood Cliffs, NJ 07632 Tele.: (201) 585-7667

Broadcast Financial Management Association, 701 Lee Street, Suite 1010, Des Plaines, IL 60016 Tele.: (312) 296-0200

Broadcast Promotion and Marketing Executives, 402 East Orange Street, Lancaster, PA 17602 Tele.: (717) 397-5727

Business Publications Audit Bureau of Circulations, 360 Park Avenue S., New York, NY 10010 Tele.: (212) 532-6880

Cable Television Administration and Marketing Society, 219 Perimeter Center Parkway, Suite 480, Atlanta, GA 30346 Tele.: (404) 399-5574

Cable Television Advertising Bureau, 757 Third Avenue, New York, NY 10017 Tele.: (212) 751-7770

Canadian Community Newspapers Association, 70588 University Avenue, Toronto, Ontario M5J 1T6 Canada Tele.: (416)598-4277

Canadian Daily Newspaper Publishers Association, 8980 Yonge Street, Suite 1100, Toronto, Ontario M4W 3P4 Canada Tele.: (416) 923-3567

Council for Cable Information, 126 E. 56th Street, New York, NY 10022 Tele.: (212) 308-7060

Directors Guild of America, 7950 Sunset Blvd., Hollywood, CA 90046 Tele.: (213) 656-1220

Inland Daily Press Association, 777 Busse Highway, Park Ridge, IL 60028-2462 Tele.: (312) 696-1140

International Circulation Managers Association, P.O. Box 17420, Dulles Airport, Washington, DC 20041 Tele.: (703) 620-9555

International Newspaper Advertising and Marketing Executives, P.O. Box 17210, Dulles Airport, Washington, DC 20041 Tele.: (703) 648-1168

International Newspaper Financial Executives, P.O. Box 17573, Dulles Airport, Washington, DC 20041 Tele.: (703) 648-1160

International Newspaper Marketing Association, P.O. Box 17422, Dulles Airport, Washington, DC 20041 Tele.: (703) 648-1094

International Typographical Union, P.O. Box 157, Colorado Springs, CO 80901 Tele.: (303) 636-2341

Magazine Publishers Association, 575 Lexington Avenue, New York, NY 10022 Tele.: (212) 752-0055

Motion Picture Association of America, 522 Fifth Avenue, New York, NY 10036 Tele.: (212) 840-6161

National Academy of Television Arts and Sciences, 110 W. 57th Street, New York, NY 10019

National Association of Broadcasters, 1771 N Street, N.W., Washington, DC 20036 Tele.: (202) 429-5386

National Association of Video Distributors, 1800 M Street, N.W., Washington, DC 20036 Tele.: (202) 452-8100

National Cable Television Association, 1724 Massachusetts Avenue, N.W., Washington, DC 20036 Tele.: (202) 775-3550

National Newspaper Association, 1627 K Street, N.W., Washington, DC 20006 Tele: (202) 466-7200

Newspaper Advertising Bureau, 1180 Avenue of the Americas, New York, NY 10036 Tele.: (212) 704-4525

Newspaper Guild, 8611 Second Avenue, Silver Springs, MD 20981 Tele.: (301) 585-2990

Newspaper Research Council, 1000 Two Ruan Center, Des Moines, IA 50309 Tele.: (515) 245-3828

Nielsen Marketing Research, Nielsen Plaza, Northbrook, IL 60062 Tele.: (212) 599-6666

Recording Industry Association of America, 888 Seventh Avenue, 9th Floor, New York, NY 10106 Tele.: (212) 765-4330

Screen Actors' Guild, 7750 Sunset Blvd., Hollywood, CA 90046 Tele.: (213) 876-3030

Standard Rate and Data Service, 3004 Glenview Road, Wilmette, IL 60091
   Tele.: (312) 256-6067
Television Information Office, 745 Fifth Avenue, New York, NY 10022
   Tele.: (212) 759-6800
Video Software Dealers Association, 1008-F, Astoria, NJ 08034
Writers' Guild of America, 8955 Beverly Blvd., Los Angeles, CA 90048
   Tele.: (213) 550-1000

PUBLICATIONS

General Media

Advertising Age. Chicago: Crain Communications, weekly.
   Advertising trade publication; annually publishes special issues on top
   media companies and top advertisers, and the state of advertising in
   various media.
Communication Industries Report. New York: Veronis, Suher & Associates,
   annual.
   Financial performance data for public companies in various media in-
   dustries.
CPI Detailed Report. Washington, DC: Department of Labor, Bureau of
   Labor Statistics, monthly.
   Reports consumer prices for products nationally and by state.
Marketing and Media Decisions. New York: Decisions Publications, monthly.
   Contains articles on changes in media trends and relates them to market-
   ing issues. Regular articles on the economy, advertising, sales, and man-
   agement issues.
Media Industry Newsletter. New York: Media Industry Newsletter, weekly.
   Reports developments in media and advertising industries, financial re-
   ports, mergers, acquisitions, closings, and ratings.
Producer Price Index. Washington, DC: Department of Labor, Bureau of
   Labor Statistics, monthly.
   Data on production prices for industries and products.
Standard Rate and Data Service. Wilmette, IL: Standard Rate and Data
   Service, monthly.
   Reports data on advertising rates, media market penetration, and so forth
   for a variety of media types.
State and Metropolitan Area Data Book. Washington, DC: Department of
   Commerce, Bureau of the Census.
   Provides demographic and economic data for states, metropolitan areas,
   and major cities.
Christopher H. Sterling and Timothy R. Haight, *The Mass Media: Aspen
   Institute Guide to Communication Industry Trends.* New York: Praeger
   Publisher, 1978.
   Historical and trend data for books, newspapers, magazines, motion
   pictures, sound recordings, radio, television, cable.

Survey of Buying Power. New York: Sales & Marketing Management, annual.
Economic and demographic data on states, metropolitan areas, and major
cities.

Audio and Visual Recordings

Billboard. New York: Billboard Publications, weekly.
Reports developments and trends in music and home video industries.
Radio & Records. Los Angeles: Radio & Records, weekly.
Covers the radio and recording industries and the interplay between the
two media forms.
Video Forecaster. Cherry Hill, NJ: Video Software Dealers Association.
Reports demand for sales and rental of video products, the status of
competition among dealers, and sales figures.
Video Marketing Newsletter. Hollywood, CA: Video Marketing Newsletter,
twice monthly.
News of the video product industry, including trends, new products, and
so forth.

Books

Publisher's Weekly. New York: Cahners Publishing, weekly.
News of book publishing, trends, sales, and marketing strategies.

Broadcasting

Arbitron Ratings. New York: Arbitron Ratings Co., quarterly.
Audience data for television and radio markets.
Birch Ratings Data for Radio Markets. Englewood Cliffs, NJ: Birch Radio,
quarterly.
Audience data for radio markets.
Broadcast Stats. Carmel, CA: Paul Kagan Associates, monthly.
Reports monthly financial data on broadcast properties.
Broadcasting/Cablecasting. Washington, DC: Broadcasting Publications,
weekly.
Reports regulatory and other aspects of broadcast industries including
station sales and industry trends.
Broadcasting/Cablecasting Yearbook. Washington, DC: Broadcasting
Publications, annual.
Reviews programming suppliers, broadcast and cablecast markets and
stations, sizes of markets, and demographics.
Duncan's Radio Market Guide. Kalamazoo, MI: Duncan's American Media,
annual.
Provides financial histories and information on competitors in 200 radio
markets, as well as geographic and demographic information.

Electronic Media. Chicago, IL: Crain Publications, weekly.
Reports development in television, radio, and cable, including sales, programming, and ratings data.

Investing in Radio. Washington, DC: Broadcast Investment Analysts, Inc., annual.
Market and station information including sales, formats, rankings, power, and ownership, as well as cross-market analyses of growth including demographic and financial growth rates and revenue statistics.

Investing in Television. Washington, DC: Broadcast Investment Analysts, Inc., annual.
Market and station information including sales, formats, rankings, power, and ownership, as well as cross-market analyses of growth including demographic and financial growth rates and revenue statistics.

A. C. Nielsen Co. Ratings Data for Broadcast and Cable Media. Northbrook, IL: A. C. Nielsen Co., quarterly.
Audience data and characteristics in broadcasting and cablecasting markets.

Radio & Records. Los Angeles: Radio & Records, weekly.
Covers the radio and recording industries and the interplay between the two media forms.

Radio Facts. New York: Radio Advertising Bureau, annual.
Reports data on radio audiences, advertising sales, and radio markets.

Radio Financial Report. Washington, DC: National Association of Broadcasters, annual.
Reports revenues and expenses for radio stations by market, station size, frequency, programming type.

Ratings Report and Directory. Los Angeles: Radio & Records, annual.
Directory of radio-oriented firms, top stations in various formats, and market information.

Television Digest. Washington, DC: Television Digest, weekly.
Trade journal that covers finance, ownership, ratings, and other developments in television and electronics industries.

Television and Cable Factbook. Washington, DC: Warren Publishing, annual.
Authoritative reference for TV, cable, and electronics industries. Contains directory of and information on all TV and cable facilities in the U.S.

Television/Radio Age. New York: Television Editorial Corp., biweekly.
Data on television and radio industries including reports on programming and station changes and trends.

Cable

Broadcasting/Cablecasting Yearbook. Washington, DC: Broadcasting Publications, annual.
Reviews programming suppliers, broadcast and cablecast markets and stations, sizes of markets, and demographics.

Cablevision. Denver, CO: International Thomson Communications, biweekly.
Information on sales, marketing, advertising, and cable firms for cable
television managers.

The Kagan Cable TV Financial Databook. Carmel, CA: Paul Kagan
Associates, annual.
Data on cable television firms and programmers, including financial
records, growth rates, ownership and debt data for private and public
firms.

Multichannel News. New York: Fairchild Publications, weekly.
Covers cable, pay cable, and broadcast television, including financial
news, costs, franchising information, and programming developments.

Television and Cable Factbook. Washington, DC: Warren Publishing Co.,
annual.
Authoritative reference for TV, cable, and electronics industries. Contains
directory of and information on all TV and cable facilities in the U.S.

Magazines

ABC Magazine Trend Report. Chicago: Audit Bureau of Circulation, annual.
Reports circulation and cost trends for consumer magazines.

Circulation: Annual Circulation and Penetration Analysis of Print Media.
Malibu, CA: American Newspaper Markets, annual.
Reports by state, county, and market areas the circulation and penetration
of major newspapers and monthly magazines.

Folio. Stamford, CT: Hanson Publishing Group, monthly.
Reports on publishing issues, problems, and trends aimed at magazine
managers.

The Gallagher Report. New York: Gallagher Report, weekly.
Focuses on marketing, advertising, sales, and management issues for
magazine executives.

Motion Pictures

Hollywood Reporter. Hollywood: Hollywood Reporter, daily.
Covers business developments and entertainment aspects of film and
television production.

Variety. New York: Cahners Publishing, weekly.
Reports sales and receipts data for current films as well as information on
motion picture industry developments and trends and some developments
in TV and music industries.

Newspapers

Audit Bureau of Circulation Audits. Chicago, IL: Audit Bureau of Circulation,
quarterly and annual.
Audited newspaper circulation data for individual markets nationwide.

Circulation: Annual Circulation and Penetration Analysis of Print Media.
Malibu: CA.: American Newspaper Markets, annual.
Reports by state, county, and market areas the circulation and penetration of daily newspapers.

Editor & Publisher. New York: Editor & Publisher, weekly.
Weekly summary of legal, economic, technological, and other developments in the newspaper industry.

Editor & Publisher International Yearbook. New York: Editor & Publisher, annual.
Provides annual summary of newspaper statistics and listings of papers and their staffs, news services, suppliers.

Editor & Publisher Market Guide. New York: Editor & Publisher, annual.
Provides economic, business, and demographic data on daily newspaper markets.

Facts About Newspapers. Reston, VA: American Newspaper Publishers Association, annual.
Compiles circulation, advertising, ownership, labor, and other statistics for the U.S. and Canadian newspaper industries.

Inland Daily Press Association Cost and Revenue Study. Park Ridge, IL: Inland Daily Press Association, annual.
Contains survey data on operating costs and revenues for 300 newspapers.

Key Facts: Newspapers, Consumers, Advertising. New York: Newspaper Advertising Bureau, annual.
Compiles data on newspaper advertising readership, costs, effects, and volume.

Presstime. Reston, VA: American Newspaper Publishers Association, monthly.
Reports on industry trends and data on specific problems and issues related to topics of articles.

GLOSSARY

Advantages A type of government intervention in economics, such as preferred treatment for a company or industry by government agencies or reduced prices for government services.

Allocation The process of determining who gets the resources, goods, or services that are available in a society.

Average Physical Product Indicates the average contribution that any one unit of input makes to overall output.

Capital The financial sum of all wealth that is increased when resources are used for the creation of goods and services. *Capital Lending* The process of lending capital to firms and individuals for a fee that will be repaid in addition to the capital that is lent. *Capital Investing* The process of contributing capital to a firm for part ownership of that firm.

Centrally Planned Economy An economic system in which allocative decisions are made by centralized authorities.

Competition Rivalry of buyers and sellers in the market. Buyers compete with sellers, buyers compete with buyers, and sellers compete with sellers. *Intramedia Competition* Competition between units of the same medium. *Intermedia Competition* Competition between units of different media or between media industries.

Concentration The degree to which the largest companies in the same product/service and geographic market control the economic activities in that market.

Concentration of Ownership The degree to which activities of an industry or related industries are owned or controlled by leading firms.

Consumption The use of resources, goods, or services to satisfy wants and needs.

Corporation A business firm organized with limited legal liability for the owners of its shares. *Publicly owned corporations* are firms whose shares are sold on stock exchanges. *Privately owned corporations* are those whose stock is not publicly traded; they tend to be owned by a smaller number of shareholders.

Cost The value that is given up for producing a good or service. This value can be measured in terms of both financial expenses and opportunities not selected. *Average cost* is cost of output spread evenly across each unit of input. *Marginal cost* is the cost of the last input made as a means of increasing output. *Long-run cost* encompasses both fixed and variable inputs and analyses of full cost and output over time. *Short-run cost* focuses on inputs and output in the short-term, with a particular emphasis on variable inputs. *Opportunity cost* is the implicit cost of the best forgone alternative to producing the product chosen.

Demand A measure of the quantity of a good or service that consumers are willing to purchase at a given price. See *Elasticity of Demand.*

Distribution Economics A type of economic analysis in which distribution rather than production factors are the focus. Used in analysis of distribution of public goods and a few private goods.

Dual Product Market A situation in which a good is two separate products that the producer sells to more than one type of buyer.

Efficiency An indicator of whether the actions of firms maximize total wealth. Actions that maximize wealth are said to be efficient, while actions that do not optimize wealth result in inefficiency. *Allocative Efficiency* A condition that occurs when the market operates at optimal points that spread its benefits evenly between consumers and producers. *Technical Efficiency* A condition that exists when inputs are used most effectively to maximize output.

Elasticity of Demand A measure of the amount that demand changes when price for a good or service is changed. *Elastic demand* occurs when the change in quantity demanded is greater than the change in price. *Inelastic demand* occurs when no significant change in quantity demanded accompanies a change in price. *Unit elasticity* occurs when the change in price and quantity are the same. *Cross elasticity* measures the substitution of another similar product that occurs when price changes occur in one product.

Elasticity of Supply A measure of the amount supply changes when price for a good or service is changed. *Elastic supply* occurs when the change in supply provided is greater than the change in price. *Inelastic supply* occurs when no significant change in quantity supplied accompanies a change in price. *Unit elasticity* occurs when the change in price and quantity supplied are the same.

Equilibrium The point at which the quantity of a product available and the price at which it is available meet on both the supply and demand curves.

Equity A welfare economics concept that describes the distribution of total wealth among producers and consumers so that it provides the greatest social benefit. The term is also used to describe the value of the ownership of a firm.

Externalities A term used to describe the results of market activities outside the market itself. Such results may be beneficial or harmful.

Geographic Market Defines the boundaries in which producers or sellers conduct trade for the products/services they offer.

Goods Commodities produced and exchanged for trade in the marketplace. *Private goods* are those that are purchased and consumed by a single individual or firm and diminish the supply of the goods available to others. *Public goods* can be acquired by many individuals or firms without diminishing the availability to others, such as a television broadcast.

Good/Service Market Distinguishes the type of good or service offered for trade by producers or sellers.

Growth An increase in output or value.

Income A financial term indicating funds available to the company after basic operating expenses are paid. Contrast with *Revenue*.

Indifference A consumer choice model based on the idea that consumers make choices among a variety of products and services and maximize satisfaction in creating a mix of consumption. Consumers are said to be indifferent to each good or service, and the quantity of each product may be varied to achieve maximum utility.

Inputs Those factors necessary to create a product or service. *Fixed inputs* are those whose quantities cannot be varied but must be present, such as equipment and buildings. *Variable inputs* are varied to achieve different levels of output. These inputs include labor and raw materials.

Interest The cost of using lent capital.

Intervention Government activities in economic markets, both at the macroeconomic level and the microeconomic level. Intervention in industries generally occurs through regulation, advantages, and subsidies.

Labor A factor of production contributed by the work of humans.

Land A factor of production that encompasses real estate and natural resources such as minerals.

Macroeconomics The branch of economics devoted to studying the economy as a whole and major aggregate issues such as employment, growth, and inflation.

Marginal Physical Product The additional output that results from the last input added.

Market Group of sellers and buyers wishing to engage in trade for products or services. See *Geographic Market* and *Good/Service Market.*

Market Conduct The policies of firms regarding their products, prices, and competitors.

Market Economy An economic system in which allocative decisions are made based on the operations of the market.

Market Performance The results of a firm or industry's activities considered in terms of efficiency, equity, and externalities created.

Market Structure The economic features of a market, including such elements as number of buyers and sellers, product differentiation, barriers to entry, and concentration.

Microeconomics The branch of economics concerned with economic activities at the market level.

Mixed Economy An economic system that combines elements of market and centrally planned economies.

Monopolistic Competition A market structure in which there are a number of sellers of similar, but differentiated, products and services competing.

Monopoly A market structure in which a single seller of a product exists and controls the market.

Needs Items that individuals and society must satisfy to ensure subsistence and survival or that are required to produce a good or service.

Oligopoly A market structure in which competition exists among a small number of producers of similar products and services.

Outputs The end good or service created by producers for consumers.

Perfect Competition A market structure in which there are many sellers for a homogeneous product or service.

Principal The actual amount of money provided or received by a firm as lent capital.

Product Supply The amount of a good or service made available for consumption by a producer or producers. See *Supply.*

Profit The return received by a producer. *Normal profit* is the minimal financial and individual reward that keeps a producer operating. *Pure profit* is the return beyond the minimum necessary to keep a firm operating and represents the return beyond expenditures that is commonly called "profit."

Regulation A type of government intervention in which market structure, conduct, or performance is determined by state apparatuses.

Resources Inanimate and animate items that can be used for producing goods and services.

Return The profit received from operation. Used as a financial performance measure, usually in comparison to overall sales, assets, investment, or equity.

Revenue Funds received from the sale or rental of goods and services. Contrast with *Income. Average Revenue* The average amount of revenue that the sale of any one unit of output made to overall revenue. *Marginal Revenue* The additional revenue that resulted from the last output sold.

Scale Relates to the size of a firm or its output. *Economies of scale* exist when long-run average costs (LRAC) decline as output and plant size increase. *Diseconomies of scale* occur when LRAC increase as output and plant size increase. *Returns to scale* indicate the relationship between proportionate changes in all inputs and output in the long-run. These returns may increase, decrease, or remain constant.

Services Work done for others to serve their needs.

Stock Shares of a corporation that are sold.

Subsidy A type of government intervention in which cash transfers are made to firms.

Substitutability The ability of one product or service to be substituted for another if consumers choose to for reasons of price, quality, or availability.

Substitute A product or service that can be used in place of another product or service to satisfy a want or need.

Supply The quantity of a product that producers will sell at a given price.

Surplus Value The additional value imparted to goods and services through labor.

Taxation A type of government intervention in which additional costs are added to market transactions to fund government activities or to penalize for externalities.

Theory of Relative Constancy Asserts that consumers' spending for media remains a constant proportion of total consumer spending and that new media induce consumers to reallocate funds spent for media rather than to reallocate total spending patterns.

Umbrella Competition A market structure in which different layers of the same medium exist in the same market, claiming smaller markets under the umbrella of a large unit of the medium that covers the entire market (typically a metropolitan area).

Util A unit of measure used in determining the utility of goods and services.

Utility Intangible consumer satisfaction from goods and services that is a component in the determination of value. *Ordinal utility* is based on a rank ordering of consumer preference. *Cardinal utility* is a measure of satisfaction based on some numerically measurable factor. *Marginal utility* indicates the additional satisfaction achieved by consuming additional units of a good or service.

Value The worth of a commodity or service, indicated by its ability to command money or other goods in exchange for the commodity or service in the market. Values change and fluctuate over time.

Wants Items that individuals and society desire to improve the quality of their lives or to gain nonsubsistence goods or services.

Welfare Economics A type of analysis concerned with public welfare as evidenced by market performance in the study of industries and firms.

EARLY CONTRIBUTIONS
TO MEDIA ECONOMICS
LITERATURE

BELSON, W. A. (1961) "Effects of television on the reading and buying of newspapers and magazines." *Public Opinion Quarterly* 25 (Fall): 366-381.

CORDEN, W. M. (1952-53) "The maximization of profit by a newspaper." *Review of Economic Studies* 20: 181-190.

CURRIER, F. (1960) "Economic theory and its application to newspapers." *Journalism Quarterly* 37 (Spring): 255-258.

FERGUSON, J. M. (1963) *The Advertising Rate Structure in the Daily Newspaper Industry.* Englewood Cliffs, NJ: Prentice-Hall.

GERALD, J. E. (1956) *The British Press Under Government Economic Controls.* Minneapolis: University of Minnesota Press.

GERALD, J. E. (1958) "Economic research and the mass media." *Journalism Quarterly* 35 (Winter): 49-55.

HELLMUTH, W. F. (1961) "The motion picture industry," pp. 393-429 in W. Adams (ed.) *The Structure of American Industry: Some Case Studies* (3rd ed.). New York: Macmillan.

KREPS, T. J. (1961) "The newspaper industry," pp. 509-532 in W. Adams (ed.) *The Structure of American Industry: Some Case Studies* (3rd ed.). New York: Macmillan.

LEVIN, H. J. (1958) "Economic structure and the regulation of television." *Quarterly Journal of Economics* 72 (August): 445-446.

MALONE, J. R. (1951) "Economic-technical bases for newspaper diversity." *Journalism Quarterly* 28 (Summer): 315-326.

PETERSON, T., J. W. JENSEN, and W. RIVERS (1965) *The Mass Media and Modern Society.* New York: Holt, Rinehart and Winston.

RAY, R. H. (1951) "Competition in the newspaper industry." *Journal of Marketing* 43 (April): 444-456.

RAY, R. H. (1952) "Economic forces as factors in daily newspaper concentration." *Journalism Quarterly* 29 (Winter): 31-42.

REDDAWAY, W. B. (1963) "The economics of newspapers." *Economic Journal* 73: 201-218.

SIEBERT, F. S. (1952) *Freedom of the Press in England, 1465-1776.* Urbana, IL: University of Illinois Press.

SMITH, C. (1977) *The Press, Politics and Patronage: The American Government's Use of Newspapers, 1789-1875.* Athens, GA: University of Georgia Press.

SMYTHE, D. W. (1960) "On the political economy of communications." *Journalism Quarterly* 37 (Autumn): 563-572.

SMYTHE, D. W. (1962) "Time, market and space factors in communication economics." *Journalism Quarterly* 39 (Winter): 3-14.
TIJMSTRA, L. F. (1959-1960) "The challenge of TV to the press: The impact of television on advertising revenues and circulations of newspapers." *Journal of Broadcasting* 4 (Winter): 3-13.

REFERENCES

ARDOIN, B. (1973) "A comparison of newspapers under joint printing contracts." *Journalism Quarterly* 50 (Summer): 340-347

BAER, W. S., H. GELLER, J. GRUNDFEST, and K. POSSNER (1974) *Concentration of Mass Media Ownership: Assessing the State of Current Knowledge*. Santa Monica, CA: Rand.

BAGDIKIAN, B. H. (1987) *The Media Monopoly* (2nd ed.). Boston: Beacon.

BARNETT, S. R. (1969) "Statement of Stephen R. Barnett." U.S. Congress, House committee on the Judiciary, Newspaper Preservation Act. Hearings before the Antitrust subcommittee on H.R. 279 and related bills, 91st Congress, 1st session, 247-267.

BARNETT, S. R. (1980) "Monopoly games — where failures win big." *Columbia Journalism Review* (May/June): 40-47.

BARWIS, G. L. (1980) "The newspaper preservation act: A retrospective analysis." *Newspaper Research Journal* 1: 27-38.

BATES, B. J. (1988) "The impact of deregulation on television station prices." *Journal of Media Economics* 1: 5-22.

BEHARRELL, P. and G. PHILO (eds.) (1977) *Trade Unions and Media*. London: Macmillan.

BELL, J. F. (1967) *A History of Economic Thought* (2nd ed.). New York: Ronald House.

BIGMAN, S. (1948) "Rivals in conformity: A study of two competing dailies." *Journalism Quarterly* 25 (Summer): 127-131.

BLANKENBURG, W. B. (1980) "Determinants of pricing of advertising in weeklies." *Journalism Quarterly* 57 (Autumn): 663-668.

BLANKENBURG, W. B. (1982) "Newspaper ownership and control of circulation to increase profits." *Journalism Quarterly* 59 (Winter): 390-398.

BLANKENBURG, W. B. (1983) "A newspaper chain's pricing behavior." *Journalism Quarterly* 60 (Spring): 275-280.

BLAU, R. T., R. C. JOHNSON, and K. J. KSOBEICH (1976) "Determinants of TV station economic value." *Journal of Broadcasting* 20: 197-207.

BLOCH, H. and M. WIRTH (1984) "The demand for pay services on cable television." *Information Economics and Policy* 1: 311-332.

BLOOMFIELD, E. (1978) "Media cross-ownership, newspaper chains, competition, and daily newspaper advertising rates." Ph.D. Dissertation, University of Rochester.

BRENNAN, T. (1988) "An economic look at taxing home audio taping." *Journal of Broadcasting and Electronic Media* 32 (Winter): 89-103.

BROWN, R. D. (1967) "Market behavior of daily newspapers." Ph.D. Dissertation, University of Illinois.

BUSTERNA, J. (1978) "Ownership, CATV, and the quality of local television news." Paper presented to the annual meeting of the Association for Education in Journalism, Seattle, WA (August 15).

BUSTERNA, J. (1980) "Ownership, CATV, and expenditures for local television news." *Journalism Quarterly* 57 (Summer): 287-291.

BUSTERNA, J. (1987) "The cross-elasticity of demand for national newspaper advertising." *Journalism Quarterly* 64 (Summer-Autumn): 346-351.

BUSTERNA, J. (1988a) "Antitrust in the 1980s: An analysis of 45 newspaper actions." *Newspaper Research Journal* 9 (Winter): 25-36.

BUSTERNA, J. (1988b) "Concentration and the industrial organization model," pp. 35-53 in R. G. Picard, J. P. Winter, M. McCombs, and S. Lacy (eds.) *Press Concentration and Monopoly: New Perspectives on Newspaper Ownership and Operation.* Norwood, NJ: Ablex.

BUSTERNA, J. (1988c) "Newspaper JOAs and the logic of predation." *Communications and the Law* 10 (April): 3-17.

BUSTERNA, J. (1988d) "Television station ownership effects on programming and idea diversity: Baseline data." *Journal of Media Economics* 1 (Fall): 63-74.

BYRON, C. (1986) *The Fanciest Dive.* New York: W. W. Norton.

CANDUSSI, D. and J. P. WINTER (1988) "Monopoly and content in Winnipeg," pp. 139-145 in R. G. Picard, J. P. Winter, M. McCombs, and S. Lacy (eds.) *Press Concentration and Monopoly: New Perspectives on Newspaper Ownership and Operation.* Norwood, NJ: Ablex.

CARLSON, J. H. (1982) "Newspaper preservation act: A critique." *Indiana Law Review* 46: 392-412.

CHAN-OLMSTED, S. and B. R. LITMAN (1988) "Antitrust and horizontal mergers in the cable industry." *Journal of Media Economics* 1 (Fall): 3-28.

CHARETTE, M. F., C. L. BROWN-JOHN, W. I. ROMANOW, and W. C. SODERLUND (1983) "Effects of chain acquisitions and terminations on advertising rates of Canadian newspapers." Paper presented to the annual meeting of the Canadian Communication Association, University of British Columbia, B.C., Canada (June).

CHEEN, B. B. (1986) *Fair Market Value of Radio Stations: A Buyers' Guide.* Washington, DC: National Association of Broadcasters.

CHERINGTON, P. W., L. V. HIRSCH, and R. BRANDWEIN (1971) *Television Station Ownership: A Case Study of Federal Agency Regulation.* New York: Hastings House.

CHILDERS, T. L. and D. M. KRUGMAN (1987) "The competitive environment of pay per view." *Journal of Broadcasting and Electronic Media* 87 (Summer): 335-342.

CLARK, J. (1976) "Circulation increase despite higher subscription rates." *Editor and Publisher* (February 4): 32.

COMANOR, W. S. and B. M. MITCHELL (1971) "Cable television and the impact of regulation." *Bell Journal of Economics and Management Science* 2: 154-212.

COMPAINE, B. M. (1979) *Who Owns the Media? Concentration of Ownership in the Mass Communications Industry.* White Plains, NY: Knowledge Industry.

COMPAINE, B. M. (1985) "The expanding base of media competition." *Journal of Communication* 35 (Summer): 81-96.

CONANT, M. (1978) *Antitrust in the Motion Picture Industry.* New York: Arno.

CORDEN, W. M. (1952-53) "The maximization of profit by a newspaper." *Review of Economic Studies* 20: 181-190.

DERTOUZOUS, J. N. and T. H. QUINN (1985) *Bargaining Responses to the Technology Revolution: The Case of the Newspaper Industry.* Santa Monica, CA: Rand.

DERTOUZOUS, J. N. and K. E. THORPE (1982) *Newspaper Groups: Economies of Scale, Tax Laws, and Merger Incentives.* Santa Monica, CA: Rand.

DIMMICK, J. and E. ROTHENBUHLER (1984) "The theory of niche: Quantifying competition among media industries." *Journal of Communication* 34 (Winter): 103-119.

DUCEY, R. V., D. M. KRUGMAN, and D. ECKRICH (1983) "Predicting market segments in the cable industry: The basic and pay subscribers." *Journal of Broadcasting* 27 (Spring): 155-175.

DUNCAN'S AMERICAN MEDIA (published annually) *Duncan's Radio Market Guide.* Kalamazoo, MI: Author.

FEDERAL COMMUNICATIONS COMMISSION (1975) Second report and order: 50 FCC 2nd 1046, 32 RF.R. 2nd 954, Docket No. 18110.

FERGUSON, J. M. (1983) "Daily newspaper advertising rates, local media cross-ownership, newspaper chains, and media competition." *Journal of Law and Economics* 28: 635-654.

FIELD, R. W. (1978) "Circulation price inelasticity in the daily newspaper industry." M.A. Thesis, University of Oklahoma.

FINK, C. C. (1988) *Strategic Newspaper Management.* New York: Random House.

FULLERTON, H. S. (1988) "Technology collides with relative constancy: The pattern of adoption for a new medium." *Journal of Media Economics* 1 (Fall): 75-84.

GIDE, C. and C. RIST (1979) *History of Economic Doctrines.* Wilmington, DE: International Academic.

GROTTA, G. (1971) "Consolidation of newspapers: What happens to the consumer." *Journalism Quarterly* 48 (Summer): 245-250.

GROTTA, G. (1977) "Daily newspaper circulation price inelastic for 1970-75." *Journalism Quarterly* 54 (Summer): 379-382.

GUBACK, T. (1987) "The evolution of the motion picture theatre business in the 1980s." *Journal of Communication* 37 (Spring): 60-77.

HANEY, L. H. (1949) *History of Economic Thought* (4th ed.). New York: Macmillan.

HEILBRONER, R. L. (1980) *The Worldly Philosophers* (5th ed.). New York: Simon and Schuster.

HENRY, J. B. (1985) "The economics of pay-TV media," pp. 19-55 in E. M. Noam (ed.) *Video Media Competition: Regulation, Economics, and Technology.* New York: Columbia University Press.

HOLLSTEIN, M. (1978) "Government and the press: The question of subsidies." *Journal of Communication* 29 (Autumn): 46-53.

HUSNI, S. A. (1988) "Influences on the survival of new consumer magazines." *Journal of Media Economics* 1 (Spring): 39-49.

INLAND DAILY PRESS ASSOCIATION (published annually) *IDPA Cost and Revenue Study.* Park Ridge, IL: Author.

INSTITUTE OF NEWSPAPER CONTROLLERS AND FINANCE OFFICERS (1975) *Profitability Analysis for Newspapers.* Morristown, NJ: Author.

KERTON, R. R. (1973) "Price effects of market power in the Canadian newspaper industry." *Canadian Journal of Economics* 6 (November): 602-606.

KIELBOWICZ, R. B. (1986) "Origins of the second-class mail category and the business of policymaking, 1863-1879." *Journalism Monographs* 96 (April).

KIERNAN, T. (1986) *Citizen Murdoch.* New York: Dodd, Mead.

KOENIG, A. E. (ed.) (1970) *Broadcasting and Bargaining: Labor Relations in Radio and Television.* Madison: University of Wisconsin Press.

LACY, S. (1984) "Competition among metropolitan daily, small daily, and weekly newspapers." *Journalism Quarterly* 61 (Autumn): 640-644.

LACY, S. (1985) "Monopoly metropolitan dailies and inter-city competition." *Journalism Quarterly* 62 (Autumn): 640-644.

LACY, S. (1987) "The effect of growth of radio on newspaper competition, 1920-1948." *Journalism Quarterly* 64 (Winter): 775-781.

LACY, S. (1988a) "The effect of intermedia competition on daily newspaper content." *Journalism Quarterly* 65: (Spring) 95-99.

LACY, S. (1988b) "Content of joint operation newspapers," pp. 147-160 in R. G. Picard, J. P. Winter, M. McCombs, and S. Lacy (eds.) *Press Concentration and Monopoly: New Perspectives on Newspaper Ownership and Operation.* Norwood, NJ: Ablex.

LACY, S. (1988c) "Competing in the suburbs: A research review of intercity newspaper competition." *Newspaper Research Journal* 9 (Winter): 59-68.

LANDAU, E. and J. S. DAVENPORT (1959) "Price anomalies of the mass media." *Journalism Quarterly* 36 (Summer): 291-294.

LAVINE, J. M. and D. B. WACKMAN (1988) *Managing Media Organizations.* New York: Longman.

LEAPMAN, M. (1984) *Arrogant Aussie: The Rupert Murdoch Story.* Secacus, NJ: Lyle Stuart.

LEVIN, H. J. (1971) *The Invisible Resource: Use and Regulation of the Radio Spectrum.* Baltimore: Johns Hopkins University Press.

LEVIN, H. J. (1975) "Franchise values, merit programming and policy options in television broadcasting," pp. 221-247 in R. E. Caves and M. J. Roberts (eds.) *Regulating the Product: Quality and Variety.* Cambridge, MA: Ballinger.

LEVIN, H. J. (1980) *Fact and Fancy in Television Regulation: An Economic Study of Television Alternatives.* New York: Russell Sage.

LEVY, J. and P. PITSCH (1985) "Statistical evidence of substitutability among video delivery systems," pp. 56-92 in E. M. Noam (ed.) *Video Media Competition: Regulation, Economics, and Technology.* New York: Columbia University Press.

LITMAN, B. R. (1988) "Macroeconomic foundations," pp. 3-34 in R. G. Picard, J. P. Winter, M. McCombs, and S. Lacy (eds.) *Press Concentration and Monopoly: New Perspectives on Newspaper Ownership and Operation.* Norwood, NJ: Ablex.

LITMAN, B. R. and J. BRIDGES (1986) "An economic analysis of daily newspaper performance." *Newspaper Research Journal* 7 (Spring): 9-26.

LITWAK, M. (1986) *Reel Power: The Struggle for Influence and Success in the New Hollywood.* New York: William Morrow.

MALONE, J. R. (1969) "Statement of John R. Malone." U.S. Congress, House committee on the Judiciary, Newspaper Preservation Act. Hearings before the Antitrust subcommittee on H.R. 279 and related bills, 91st Congress, 1st session, 337-344.

MARCUS, N. (1986) *Broadcast and Cable Management.* Englewood Cliffs, NJ: Prentice-Hall.

MARX, K. (1952) *Capital* (Friedrich Engels, ed.; Samuel Moore and Edward Aveling, trans.) Chicago: Encyclopedia Britannica. (Original work published 1867)

MATHEWSON, G. F. (1972) "A note on the price effects of market power in the Canadian newspaper industry." *Canadian Journal of Economics* 5: 298-301.

MAYER, M. F. (ed.) (1973) *The Film Industries.* New York: Hastings House.

McCABE, P. (1987) *Bad News at Black Rock: The Sell-Out of CBS News.* New York: Arbor House.

McCLINTICK, D. (1982) *Indecent Exposure: A True Story of Hollywood and Wall Street.* New York: William Morrow.

McCOMBS, M. E. (1972) "Mass media in the marketplace." *Journalism Monographs* 24 (August).

McCOMBS, M. E. (1988) "Concentration, monopoly, and content," pp. 129-137 in R. G. Picard, J. P. Winter, M. McCombs, and S. Lacy (eds.) *Press Concentration and Monopoly: New Perspectives on Newspaper Ownership and Operation.* Norwood, NJ: Ablex.

McGANN, A. F., J. F. RUSSELL, and J. T. RUSSELL (1983) "Variable pricing in advertising space for regional and metro magazines." *Journalism Quarterly* 60 (Summer): 269-275.

McGANN, A. F. and J. T. RUSSELL (1988) "Are broadcasters especially vulnerable to takeovers?" *Journal of Media Economics* 1 (Fall): 29-40.

NATIONAL ASSOCIATION OF BROADCASTERS (published annually) *Radio Financial Report.* Washington, DC: Author.

NATIONAL ASSOCIATION OF BROADCASTERS (1978) *NAB Guide to Investment in Broadcast Properties.* Washington, DC: Author.

NIEBAUER, W. E., Jr. (1984) "Effects of Newspaper Preservation Act on the suburban press." *Newspaper Research Journal* 5 (Spring): 41-49.

NIXON, R. B. and R. L. JONES (1956) "The content of non-competitive vs. competitive newspapers." *Journalism Quarterly* 33 (Summer): 299-315.

NOAM, E. M. (1985a) "Economies of scale in cable television: A multiproduct analysis," pp. 93-120 in E. M. Noam (ed.) *Video Media Competition: Regulation, Economics, and Technology.* New York: Columbia University Press.

NOAM, E. M. (ed.) (1985b) *Video Media Competition: Regulation, Economics, and Technology.* New York: Columbia University Press.

NOLL, R. G., M. J. PECK, and J. J. McGOWAN (1973) *Economic Aspects of Television Regulation.* Washington, DC: Brookings Institute.

NORRIS, V. (1982) "Consumer magazine prices and the mythical advertising subsidy." *Journalism Quarterly* 59 (Summer): 205-211.

NORTON, S. W. and W. NORTON, Jr. (1986) "Economies of scale and the new technology of daily newspapers: A survivor analysis." *Quarterly Review of Economics and Business* 26 (Summer): 66-83.

O'DONNELL, L. B., C. HAUSMAN, and P. BENOIT (1989) *Radio Station Operations.* Belmont, CA: Wadsworth.

OWEN, B. M. (1975) *Economics and Freedom of Expression: Media Structure and the First Amendment.* Cambridge, MA: Ballinger.

OWEN, B. M. (1978) "Structural approaches to the problem of TV network economic dominance." *Center for the Study of Business Regulation Paper Series* 27. Durham, NC: Duke University, Graduate School of Business Administration.

OWEN, B. M., J. H. BEEBE, and W. G. MANNING, Jr. (1974) *Television Economics.* Lexington, MA: D.C. Heath.

PAPER, L. J. (1987) *Empire: William S. Paley and the Making of CBS.* New York: St. Martin's.

PARK, R. E. (1970) *Potential Impact of Cable Growth on Television Broadcasting.* Santa Monica, CA: Rand.

PARK, R. E. (1971) *Prospects for Cable in the 100 Largest Television Markets.* Santa Monica, CA: Rand.

PAUL KAGAN ASSOCIATES (published annually) *Broadcast Stats.* Carmel, CA: Author.

PICARD, R. G. (1982) "Rate setting and competition in newspaper advertising." *Newspaper Research Journal 3* (April): 23-13.

PICARD, R. G. (1985a) "Patterns of state intervention in western press economics." *Journalism Quarterly* 62 (Spring): 1-9.

PICARD, R. G. (1985b) *The Press and the Decline of Democracy: The Democratic Socialist Response in Public Policy.* Westport, CT: Greenwood.

PICARD, R. G. (1985c) "Pricing behavior in monopoly newspapers: Ad and circulation differences in joint operating and single newspaper monopolies, 1972-1982." *LSU School of Journalism Research Bulletin.*

PICARD, R. G. (1986) "Pricing in competing and monopoly newspapers, 1972-1982." *LSU School of Journalism Research Bulletin.*

PICARD, R. G. (1987) "Evidence of a failing newspaper under the Newspaper Preservation Act." *Newspaper Research Journal* 9 (Fall): 73-82.

PICARD, R. G. (1988a) "Measures of concentration in the daily newspaper industry." *Journal of Media Economics* 1 (Spring): 61-74.

PICARD, R. G. (1988b) "Pricing behavior of newspapers," pp. 55-69 in R. G. Picard, J. P. Winter, M. McCombs, and S. Lacy (eds.) *Press Concentration and Monopoly: New Perspectives on Newspaper Ownership and Operation.* Norwood, NJ: Ablex.

PICARD, R. G. (1988c) "It's time to revise the Newspaper Preservation Act." *Editor & Publisher* (September 24): 48+.

PICARD, R. G., J. P. WINTER, M. McCOMBS, and S. LACY (eds.) (1988) *Press Concentration and Monopoly: New Perspectives on Newspaper Ownership and Operation.* Norwood, NJ: Ablex.

PIGOU, A. C. (1932) *Economics of Welfare.* London: Macmillan.

ROSSE, J. N. (1967) "Daily newspaper monopoly, competition and economies of scale." *American Economic Review* 57: 522-533.

ROSSE, J. N. (1975) "Economic limits of press responsibility." *Studies in Industry Economics* 56. Stanford, CA: Stanford University, Department of Economics.

ROSSE, J. N. (1980) "The decline of direct newspaper competition." *Journal of Communication* 30 (Spring): 65-71.

ROTHENBERG, J. (1962) "Consumer sovereignty and the economics of TV programming." *Studies in Public Communication* 4 (Fall): 45-54.

SCHARFF, E. (1988) *Worldly Power: The Making of the Wall Street Journal.* New York: New American Library.

SCHILLER, H. I. (1981) *Who Knows? Information in the Age of the Fortune 500.* Norwood, NJ: Ablex.

SCHUMPETER, J. A. (1965) *Ten Great Economists.* New York: Oxford University Press.

SCRIPPS, C. E. (1965) *Economic Support of Mass Communication in the United States, 1929-1964.* Cincinnati: Scripps-Howard Research.

SEGLOW, P. (1978) *Trade Unionism in Television: A Case Study in the Development of White Collar Militancy.* Farnborough, U.K.: Saxon House.

SMITH, A. (1952) *An Inquiry into the Nature and Cause of the Wealth of Nations.* Chicago: Encyclopedia Britannica. (Original work published 1776)

SMITH, A. (1977) "Subsidies and the press in Europe." *Political and Economic Planning* 569.

STEINER, P. O. (1952) "Program patterns and preferences, and the workability of competition in radio broadcasting." *Quarterly Journal of Economics* 66 (May): 194-223.

UNITED STATES V. CITIZEN PUBLISHING CO., 280 F. Supp. 978 (D. Ariz. 1968), aff'd, 394 U.S. 131 (1969).

UNITED STATES V. TIMES MIRROR CO., 274 F. Supp. 6060 (C.D. Cal. 1967), aff'd per curiam, 390 U.S. 718 (1968).

VERONIS, SUHLER & ASSOCIATES (published annually) *Communications Industry Report.* New York: Author.

WEAVER, D. H. and L. E. MULLINS (1975) "Content and format characteristics in competing newspapers." *Journalism Quarterly* 52 (Summer): 257-264.

WHITE, L. J. (1985) "Antitrust and video markets: The merger of Showtime and the Movie Channel as a case study," pp. 363-383 in E. M. Noam (ed.) *Video Media Competition: Regulation, Economics, and Technology.* New York: Columbia University Press.

WIRTH, M. O. (1986) "Economic barriers to entering media industries in the United States," pp. 423-442 in M. McLaughlin (ed.) *Communication Yearbook 9.* Beverly Hills, CA: Sage.

WIRTH, M. O. and J. A. WOLLERT (1984) "The effects of market structure on television news pricing." *Journal of Broadcasting* 28 (Spring): 215-225.

WOLPERT, S. A. and J. FRIEDMAN WOLPERT (1986) *Economics of Information.* New York: Van Nostrand Rheinhold.

YULE, A. (1988) *Fast Fade: David Putnam, Columbia Pictures and the Battle for Hollywood.* New York: Delacorte.

INDEX

ABOUT THE AUTHOR

ROBERT G. PICARD is editor of the *Journal of Media Economics* and associate professor and director of the Communication Industries Management Program at Emerson College in Boston.

He was senior editor of the book *Press Concentration and Monopoly: New Perspectives on Newspaper Ownership and Operation* (Ablex, 1988), and the author of *The Press and the Decline of Democracy: The Democratic Socialist Response in Public Policy* (Greenwood, 1985) and *The Ravens of Odin: The Press in the Nordic Nations* (Iowa State University Press, 1988). He has written more than 100 articles on media issues for publications such as *Journalism Quarterly, Political Communication and Persuasion, Journal of Communication Inquiry, Newspaper Research Journal, Journal of Media Economics, European Studies Journal, International Press Institute Report, Gazette, Index on Censorship, The Press, Editor and Publisher, The Quill* (Society of Professional Journalists), and *The Bulletin* (American Society of Newspaper Editors).

Picard is a member of the editorial boards of *Newspaper Research Journal, Political Communication and Persuasion, American Journalism,* and *Journal of Mass Media Ethics.*

He received his Ph.D. from the University of Missouri School of Journalism, after completing an M.A. at California State University, Fullerton, and a B.A. at Loma Linda University. Picard was formerly publications editor of the Freedom of Information Center (the national research center on controls of information), and editor of the *Ontario* (California) *Daily Report,* editor of the *Riverside* (California) *Community News,* and a reporter for the *Morning Advocate* in Baton Rouge, Louisiana.

His awards and honors include selection as one of the Outstanding Young Men in America and inclusion in *Men of Achievement, Contemporary Authors,* and the *International Who's Who in Education.* He received the Clinton F. Denman Freedom of Information Award, the Frank Luther Mott Historical Research Award, a Herrick Fellowship, an East/West Foundation Scholarship, and numerous grants for research and study from organizations including the Gannett Foundation, the Association of Alternative News Weeklies, the Council for the International Exchange of Scholars, and the Southern Regional Education Board.

He has been a consultant on media economics issues for newspapers and magazines and media labor organizations, has testified before Congress on issues involving the Newspaper Preservation Act, and has provided advice and expert testimony in cases involving antitrust issues in the newspaper and broadcasting industries and joint operating agreements in the newspaper industry. He is often consulted by the popular press and media industry publications covering issues involving media economics and public policy.